About

The Good Guide to Cornwall gives... ...is for pubs, hotels, B&Bs, restaurants... and castles, viewpoints, family fun and more....

In short **everything** you need to plan your holiday.

What's more each and every listing has a postcode, so you can find the secluded beach and the awesome view just by following your satnav.

We'll always include a website address and telephone number where possible so you can investigate further.

We've uncovered some amazing places to stay, charming pubs, exclusive restaurants and the best beaches. We list our favourites at the start of each section.

Ross Harvey

Send us a review and get a free ebook

We'd like to make The Good Guide to Cornwall even better by featuring reviews by real people. Can you help?

Have you visited any of the places featured in this guide? Would you like to have a review – your honest opinion – appear in these pages? Please email us a review at

review@thegoodguides.co.uk

If your review is featured in the next edition of this guide then we will gift you an ebook version of the good guide of your choice for free.

First published in Great Britain in 2013 by

Pepik Books

hello@pepik.com

@pepikbooks

www.pepik.com

All rights reserved. No reproduction, copy or transmission of this publication may be made without written permission. No paragraph of this publication may be reproduced, copied or transmitted save with the written permission or in a accordance with the provision of the Copyright Act 1956 (as amended). Any person who does any unauthorised act in relation to this publication may be liable to criminal prosecution and civil claims form damages.

Ross Harvey is hereby identified as the author of this work in accordance with Section 77 of the Copyright, Designs and Patents Act 1988.

Text © 2013 Ross Harvey, Claire Theyers

Contents

Cornwall... 1

Bodmin Moor: Blisland, Bodmin, Bolventor, Camelford and Liskeard...5

Tamar Valley: Calstock, Saltash, Callington and Launceston 25

North East Cornwall: Boscastle, Bude, Padstow, Port Isaac, Rock,
Wade... 41

North West Cornwall: Newquay, Mawgan Porth, Perranporth, St
Agnes, Watergate Bay.. 67

South East Cornwall: Fowey, Looe, Lostwithiel, Rame Peninsula,
Polperro and Torpoint... 85

South West Cornwall: Falmouth, Mevagissey, Penryn, St Austell and
Truro.. 109

Lizard Peninsula.. 143

St Ives and Newlyn... 159

Penzance and surrounding area..179

Penwith - The Western tip of Cornwall..195

Sources... 211

Cornwall

Cornwall is famously the land beyond England and it tapers away to a rock-hard, windswept, sun-and-showers peninsula, with a long and spectacular coastline and a uniquely mild coastal climate. Most place names bear witness to its Celtic culture and reinforce the feeling that you have arrived somewhere else.

Fifteen thousand years ago, when the last Ice Age ended, Britain was still attached to the continental landmass. During the next eight thousand years this land became inhabited, then seven thousand years ago, rising sea levels made it an island. Just over 60% of the present population are descended from these first inhabitants but in Cornwall that rises to 80%. These recent advances in genetic tracing reveal there is more than just a cultural component to Cornish 'otherness'.

The sea is central to Cornish life and is what unites the wreckers of yore, the revival of gig racing in beautiful 32-ft rowing boats, and surfing in the 'extreme sports' capital of Britain, **Newquay**, where **Fistral Beach** is a Mecca of the surfing world and the venue for the European Championships. Fishing boats still animate more ports in Cornwall than you will see elsewhere, and a feeling of romance attaches to the place.

It is 1,376 square miles in area with a population of half a million – about half that of Devon, in each case. It has correspondingly fewer pubs and great houses, but in the other categories of attraction that we cover it is at least Devon's equal, exceeding it in the number of great gardens. Beaches are the heart of a family holiday, and nowhere has a greater variety or quality. The sporty, beach-life scene on the north coast has made it a teenage magnet where all-night beach partying is another sport. If the weather drives you off the beach, there is still more than enough to entertain all age groups, and interests. Cornwall is a cornucopia of possibilities – see family attractions.

From **Rough** (pronounced 'Row') **Tor** or **Brown Willy** on **Bodmin Moor** both the Atlantic and the English Channel are visible. For those fascinated by the remains of prehistoric cultures, from Bronze Age to early Iron Age and standing stones, the area near St Ives is peculiarly rich. Only Cornwall has such amazing one-offs as **St Michael's Mount**, the **Minack** open-air theatre, the **National Maritime Museum** in Falmouth, or the **Barbara Hepworth Sculpture Garden** in St Ives. Tin mining has left a legacy of remarkable ruins and china clay mining created great white gashes in the landscape, one of which is now the site of a modern wonder – the **Eden Project**, a re-creation of the plant life of the planet with different climate zones in different bio-domes. For church-lovers, **Launceston** has a carved granite façade of such plasticity that you might think that carving granite was like making pastry. It is one of England's treasures. **St Neot's** has Britain's second most complete set of medieval glass, a veritable jewel-case of religious art with a numinous feel.

The South West Coast Path is a walkers' paradise and more than half of its 629- mile length is in Cornwall, much of it owned and well tended by the National Trust, away from roads but seldom far from a pub. For those who travel on their stomach, Cornwall has enhanced its already fine reputation. Few will need to be told of the impact the star chef Rick Stein has had on Padstow, with 'foodies' taking over where the beach crowds leave off, but good eating isn't localised – the county's three Michelin stars are well spread. It also has some delightful pubs, often with very good food, and nowhere on the coast is far from a good meal or well-priced accommodation.

Cornwall is a land of artists and writers. St Ives has the greatest concentration of artists outside London, along with galleries of the highest calibre. Daphne Du Maurier lived at Menabilly, near Fowey, and Cornwall's genius comes alive in the pages of Jamaica Inn, Rebecca and Frenchman's Creek. Virginia Woolf's acclaimed novel To the Lighthouse was inspired by Godrevy lighthouse, for she spent many childhood summers in St Ives. John Betjeman drew on the county's magic and is buried at St Enodoc, which also has a lovely golf course.

Getting there is made easy by the much improved A30, a fast road compared with the A390 but short on filling stations. Even the most pluperfect, postcard-pretty villages are not ruined in high summer, but parking can be a problem; so think longer stays in high season, while in the off-season you can get around easily enough to do a lot over a long weekend. From Penzance harbour or heliport, the Isles of Scilly have their own magic, with some delightful accommodation and even a Michelin star. For a quiet, utterly relaxing holiday they are in a class apart.

Ross Harvey

A sailing boat in the bay at St Ives

Bodmin Moor: Blisland, Bodmin, Bolventor, Camelford and Liskeard

Bodmin Moor is a gaunt and wild place, with rock outcrops heather and high tors. It has a savage bleakness in winter and a beauty all of its own in summer. It rises to 1377ft at *Brown Willy*, the highest tor on the moor, from which you can see both the north coast and the south coast of Cornwall. Guarding the moor to east and west are two historic castles - *Launceston* and *Restormel*. The moor is home to some of the finest stone-age monuments in Britain: the *Trevethy Quoit* from 3,400 BC is an imposing arrangement of six huge uprights supporting a massive capstone, the whole once covered by a mound of earth which sheltered the tombs. The *Cheesewring* is a weird formation of giant granite slabs. The *Hurlers Stone Circle* and the *Minions* are both remarkable evidence of a flourishing pre-history. *Dozmary Pool* is unremarkable except as the place where the legendary *Excalibur* was thrown.

On the southern slopes of the moor is *St Neots* where the church has glass by a 15C Flemish master. It is so excellent that even people who don't 'get' churches will feel the numinous vibes.

Bodmin, pop. C. 13,000 lies on the south west of the moor and was the county town of Cornwall until the Crown Courts moved to Truro in 1988 (Launceston was county town until 1835) It is on the route of the famous Camel Trail, a disused railway line popular with walkers, cyclists and horses, linking Wenfordbridge, Bodmin, Wadebridge and Padstow.

Just 2½ miles from Bodmin is *Lanhydrock,* the grandest house in Cornwall and the most visited house in England. Begun c1620, all except the long gallery burnt to the ground in 1881. It passed to the NT in 1953 and was rebuilt during the 1960's opening in 1969, just in time for 'Upstairs, Downstairs' on TV. It never looked back. It is an excellent day out, with or without the family.

Pencarrow 4 miles north west of Bodmin is as lush 18th century as

Cornwall gets. TV producers like it and there is much to like.

Blisland village in a cleft high in Bodmin Moor features an 11th Century church with some good 19th Century work.

Bolventor is a tiny village at the centre of the moor with the famous staging post, The Jamaica Inn as its focal point.

Camelford is a small town with a fine main square (free parking) at the north of the moor, through which flows the river Camel.

Liskeard, once an important Stannary Town (Latin *stannum* tin) where tin coinage was collected as a tax. It is a pretty town featuring Georgian and Victorian houses.

Carbilly Tor

Bodmin Moor: Blisland, Bodmin, Bolventor, Camelford and Liskeard

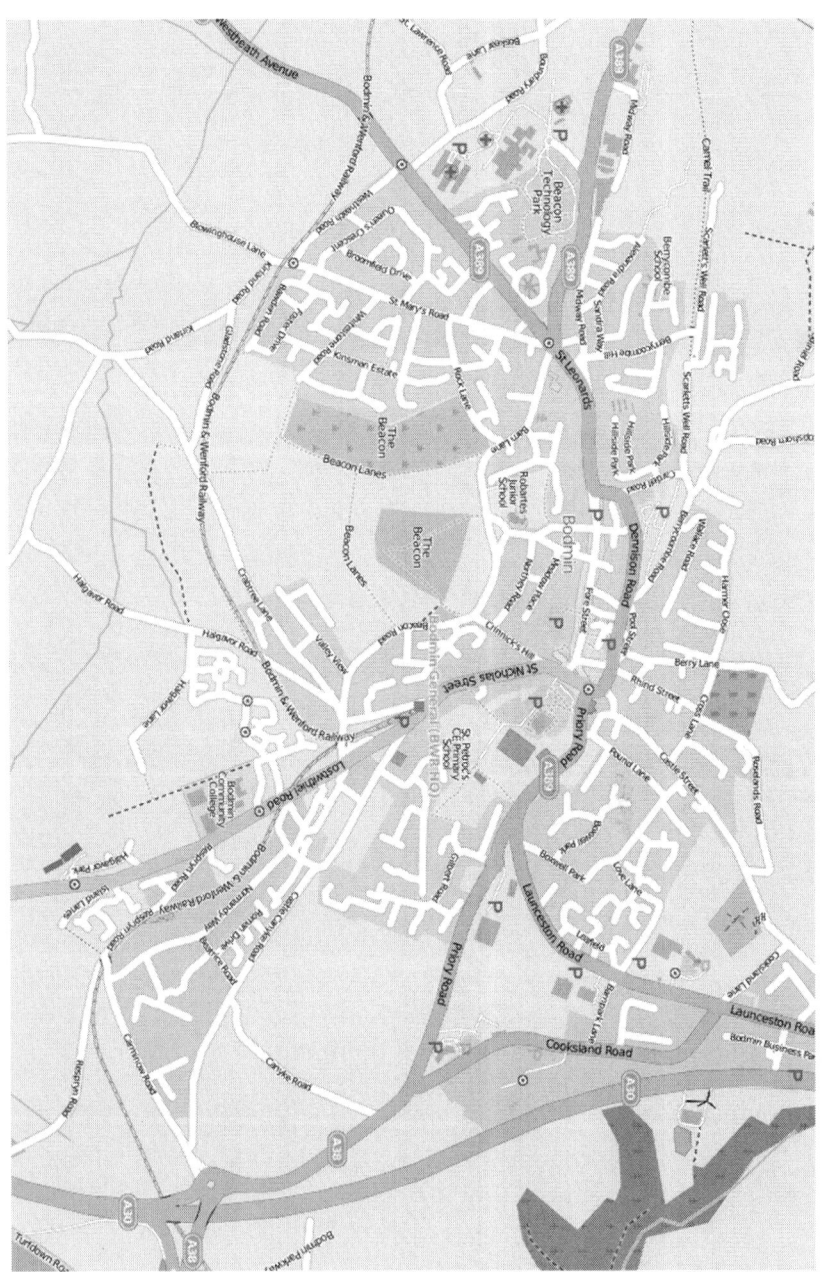

Bodmin town centre © OpenStreetMap contributors

Bodmin Moor: Blisland, Bodmin, Bolventor, Camelford and Liskeard

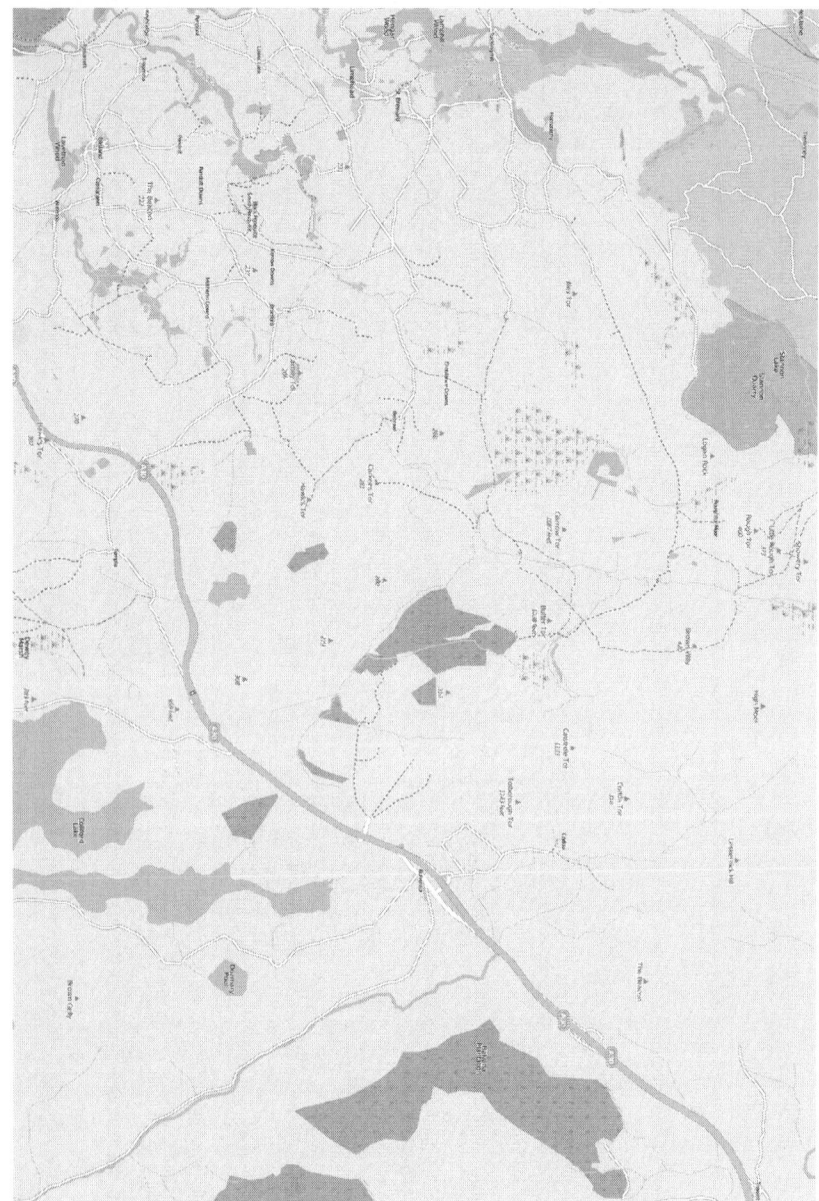

Bodmin Moor © OpenStreetMap contributors

Bodmin Moor: Blisland, Bodmin, Bolventor, Camelford and Liskeard

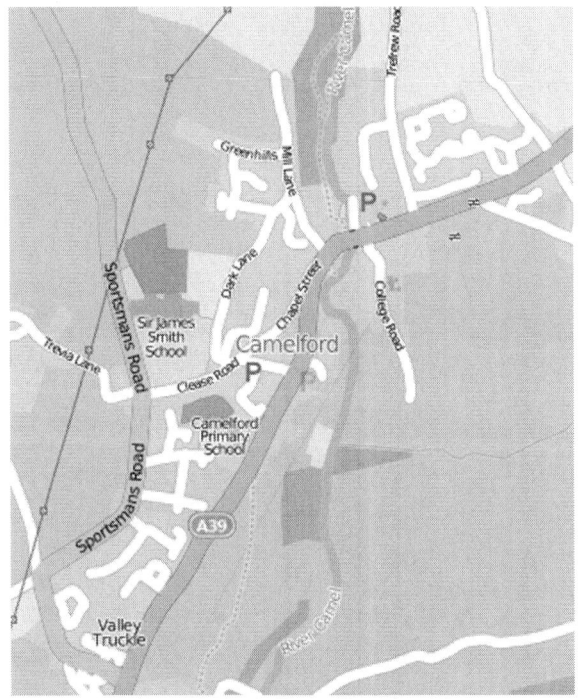

Camelford © OpenStreetMap contributors

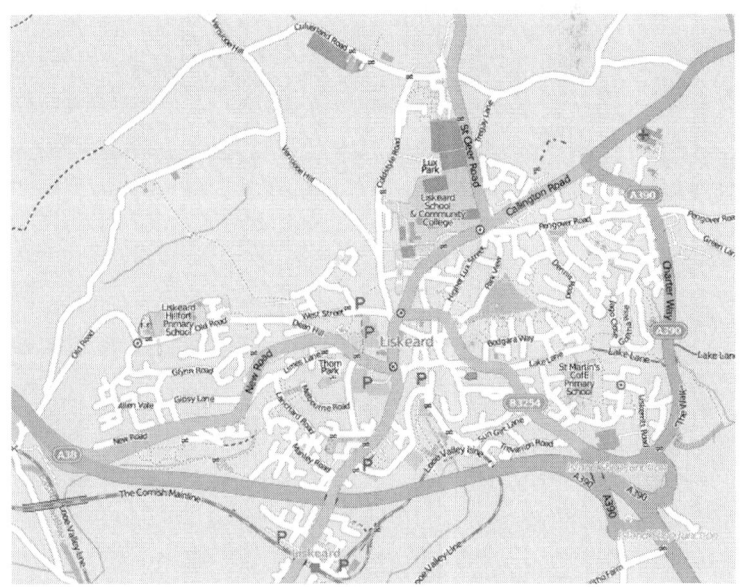

Liskeard © OpenStreetMap contributors

OUR FAVOURITES

Pendragon Country Hotel, Camelford (PL32 9XR)
HOTEL

A beautifully presented multi award winning family run country house, offering quality accommodation at its best. Sharon and Nigel offer luxury accommodation in relaxed yet sumptuous surroundings, with genuinely friendly and attentive hospitality.

Davidstow, **Camelford**, PL32 9XR
01840 261131
http://www.pendragoncountryhouse.com

BED & BREAKFAST

Interesting and highly rated B&Bs with a focus on your comfort and a warm welcome.

Higher Lank Farm B & B
St Breward, **Bodmin**, PL30 4NB
01208 850716
http://www.higherlankfarm.co.uk
Unique farm holidays for families with young children, babies and toddlers in Cornwall.

Cabilla Manor B & B
Nr Mount, **Bodmin**, PL30 4DW
01208 821224
http://www.cabilla.co.uk
A spacious Georgian farmhouse on the edge of Bodmin Moor.

Lavethan B & B
Bodmin, PL30 4QG
01208 850487
http://www.lavethan.com
Lavethan is a Grade 2* manor house.

Tremoren B & B
St Kew, **Bodmin**, PL30 3HA
01208 841790
Comfortable rooms and quiet location.

Mount Pleasant B & B
Mount, **Bodmin**, PL30 4EX
01208 821342
http://www.mountpleasantcottages.co.uk
Self-catering cottages and B&B nestling on the edge of Bodmin Moor.

Polgwyn B & B
Castle Street, **Bodmin**, PL31 2DX
01208 775533
http://www.bedknobs.co.uk
Elegant, spacious and exceedingly comfortable accommodation.

Kings Acre B & B
Camelford, PL32 9UR
01840 213561
A hidden gem.

Bokiddick Farm B & B
Lanivet, PL30 5HP
01208 831481
http://www.bokiddickfarm.co.uk
Set in a peaceful location with magnificent views of rolling countryside that is part of a nature conservation area.

Tregondale Farm B & B
Menheniot, **Liskeard**, PL14 3RG
01579 342407
http://www.tregondalefarm.co.uk
Tregondale Manor Farm is a traditional working farm in Menheniot offering farmhouse B&B and holiday cottage.

Botelet B & B
Herodsfoot, **Liskeard**, PL14 4RD
01503 220225
http://www.botelet.com
Organic farmhouse bed and breakfast • Cottages • Yurts • Meadow camping

Higher Searles Down B & B
Colliford Lake, St Neot, **Liskeard**, PL14 6QA
01208 821412
http://www.hsdown.go-plus.net/
With sweeping views down to the distant sea it offers an ideal touring base for all of Cornwall.

Penquite House B & B
Liskeard, PL14 5AQ
01579 347503
http://www.eastpenquitefarm.com
Mature gardens, unspoilt wetland, ancient Cornish hedges, a wildflower meadow, traditional orchard.

Cornish Tipi Holidays B & B
Tregeare, **St Kew**, PL30 3LW
01208 880781
http://www.cornishtipiholidays.co.uk
Stay in a canvas tipi with family or friends, living close to the earth and the rhythm of nature, an extraordinary experience.

PUBS/GASTROPUBS

Above average pubs serving quality real ale, excellent bar food or both.

Blisland Inn `PUB`
Blisland, PL30 4JK
01208 850739
http://www.bodminmoor.co.uk/blislandinn/
CAMRA's National Pub of the Year 2001.

The Crown Inn `PUB`
Lanlivery, **Bodmin**, PL30 5BT
01208 872707
http://www.wagtailinns.com/
One of the oldest pubs in Cornwall. Also offers bed and breakfast accommodation.

Bodmin Moor: Blisland, Bodmin, Bolventor, Camelford and Liskeard

RESTAURANTS

Only top notch restaurants are listed here. Cooking stars are drawn from "The Good Food Guide 2013".

St Kew Inn ★★☆☆☆☆☆☆☆☆ RESTAURANT

St Kew, **Bodmin**, PL30 3HB
01208 841259
http:///www.stkewinn.co.uk
600 year old pub with a few surprises in store.

CHURCHES

These churches all have something special and are worthy of a visit. Star ratings are from Simon Jenkin's Best Churches.

St Protus & St Hyacinth ★★★☆☆ CHURCH
N of A30 E of Bodmin, **Blisland**, PL30 4JJ

St Petroc ★★☆☆☆ CHURCH
Bodmin, PL31 2NN

St Neot ★★★★☆ CHURCH
E of Bodmin N of A38, **St Neot**, PL14 6PA

HOUSES & CASTLES

Lanhydrock House ★★★★☆ `HOUSE`
Bodmin, PL30 5AD
01208 265950
http://www.nationaltrust.org.uk/lanhydrock/
Magnificent late Victorian country house with gardens and wooded estate

Pencarrow House and Gardens ★★★☆☆ `HOUSE`
Pencarrow, **Bodmin**, PL30 3AG
01208 841369
http://www.pencarrow.co.uk/
Pencarrow House and Gardens lies at the foot of a sweeping valley between Bodmin and Wadebridge in Cornwall. The largely Georgian mansion is still owned and occupied by descendants of the family who settled there in the 1500s. Open to the public since the 1970s, Pencarrow House and Gardens is a great day out for families, history enthusiasts, nature and garden lovers, and of course the dogs.

GARDENS

Gardens listed here have been rated by the "Good Gardens Guide".

Lanhydrock ★☆☆☆☆ GARDEN

Bodmin, PL30 5AD
01208 265950
http://www.nationaltrust.org.uk/lanhydrock/
The garden is famous for spectacular magnolias, camellias and rhododendrons complementing the profusion of wild flowers.

Pencarrow House and Gardens ★☆☆☆☆ GARDEN

Washaway, **Bodmin**, PL30 3AG
01208 841369
www.pencarrow.co.uk/
Pencarrow's gardens are a combination of formal landscaping and woodland walks, with attractive planting for both garden specialists and casual walkers. Shorter and longer walking loops are available, as well as some wheelchair access.

VIEWPOINTS

Brown Willy VIEWPOINT
Camelford, PL15 7SH

Brown Willy is the highest point of Bodmin Moor and of Cornwall as a whole. It stands at 420m/1,378 ft high and both the English Channel & Atlantic can be seen from the top.

Rough Tor VIEWPOINT
Camelford, PL15 7SH

The site is composed of the tor summit and logan stone, a neolithic tor enclosure, a large number of Bronze Age hut circles, and some contemporary monuments. Its summit is 1313 ft (400m) above mean sea level, making it the second highest point in Cornwall after Brown Willy.

ARCHAEOLOGY

Trethevy Quoit ARCHAEOLOGY
Liskeard, PL14 5EJ

Spectacular Neolithic burial chamber from over 2000 BC. It is known locally as "the giant's house". Standing 9 feet (2.7 m) high, it consists of five standing stones capped by a large slab.

Bodmin Moor: Blisland, Bodmin, Bolventor, Camelford and Liskeard

FAMILY FUN

Bodmin & Wenford Railway FAMILY FUN
Steam - General Station St Nicholas Street, **Bodmin**, PL31
0845 1259678
http://www.bodminandwenfordrailway.co.uk

Bodmin Jail ★☆☆☆☆ FAMILY FUN
Berrycombe Road, **Bodmin**, PL31 2NR

http://www.bodminjail.org/
An all weather family attraction that includes a bar and restaurant, covered courtyard, with a civil and naval prison housing a museum within its walls. The jail now sits at the start of the famous Camel Trail and is the perfect alternative day out.

Lakeside Adventure Park FAMILY FUN
Wide range of attractions, **Bodmin Moor**, PL14 6PZ
01208 821469

British Cycling Museum FAMILY FUN
The Old Station at Camelford, **Camelford**, PL32 9TZ
01840 212811
http://www.chycor.co.uk/cycling-museum

NATURAL PRODUCE

Camel Valley NATURAL PRODUCE
Nanstallon, Bodmin, **Bodmin**, PL30 5LG
01208 77959
http://www.camelvalley.com
Award winning wine producer

A1 Fruiterers NATURAL PRODUCE
19 Market Place, Camelford, **Camelford**, PL32 9PB
01840 212424
http://www.a1fruiterers.co.uk
High class greengrocers

Cornish Country Meats NATURAL PRODUCE
Treverbyn Mill, St Neot, **Liskeard**, PL14 6HG
01579 320303
http://www.cornishcountrymeats.co.uk/
Venison, wild boar & beef

Cornish Orchards NATURAL PRODUCE
Duloe, **Liskeard**, PL14 4PW
01503 269007
http://www.cornishorchards.co.uk
Cornish Orchards produces quality hand crafted apple juices and ciders using the harvests of small and old orchards throughout the West Country.

Cornish cheese Company NATURAL PRODUCE
Upton Cross, **Liskeard**, PL14 5BG
01579 363660
http://www.cornishcheese.co.uk
Award wining farmhouse blue cheese

GOLF COURSES

Courses in this guide have reached a very good standard and have something special to offer the advanced and novice player alike.

Lanhydrock Golf Club ★★★★☆ GOLF
Lostwithiel Road, **Bodmin**, PL30 5AQ
01208 73600
www.lanhydrockhotel.com/
A Golf Club set in Iconic Scenery

Tamar Valley: Calstock, Saltash, Callington and Launceston

The name has the same pre-historic roots as the Thames and it forms the Devon/Cornwall boundary. Its source on Woolley Moor is only 3.7 miles from the north Cornish coast from which it flows south to the Hamoaze at Plymouth, thereby nearly making Cornwall an island. This is a clue to the character of what lies beyond.

The Tamar Valley is an area rich in beauty and history. A tranquil, blooming oasis with creeks meandering through. It's great walking country with plenty to explore. The area is full of pretty villages and bustling towns.

Callington in the west has an unusual mural trail. Kit Hill is a mile northeast of the town and rises to 333 metres (1,093 ft) with views of Dartmoor, Bodmin Moor and the River Tamar. Nearby is *Cotehele* the charming Tudor stately home on the Tamar – filled with 17th century tapestries. NT since 1947 the formal gardens around the house give to more secretive informality as they descend to the river.

Launceston, the first county town, is perched high on the Cornwall-Devon border. It is an ancient town with a 13th century castle and the amazing premier church of Cornwall. Its carved wall decoration is unparalleled in England. It almost makes granite appear as workable as plasticene. From a distance it has the outline of a Tuscan hill town – rather dramatic and worth a stop.

Saltash is located on the River Tamar and is known as the gateway to Cornwall as it connects Cornwall to Devon by road, rail and river. The spectacular rail bridge, ⅔ of a mile long and the work of I K Brunel, was opened in 1859 and was the first major link of any kind between Cornwall and the rest of England. Its impact transformed Cornwall. Artists and art lovers gathered in Newlyn and St Ives, now best seen in the Penlee Gallery in Penzance, while holiday-makers took to the beaches.

Tamar Valley: Calstock, Saltash, Callington and Launceston

Tamar Valley © OpenStreetMap contributors

Tamar Valley: Calstock, Saltash, Callington and Launceston

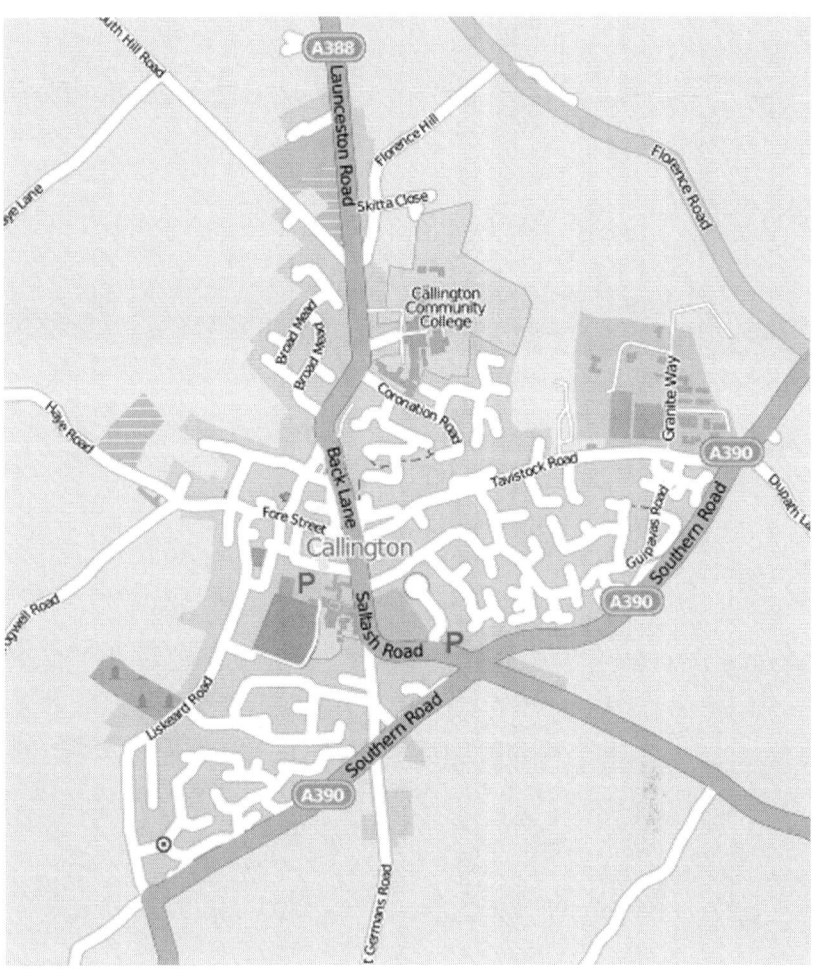

Callington © OpenStreetMap contributors

Tamar Valley: Calstock, Saltash, Callington and Launceston

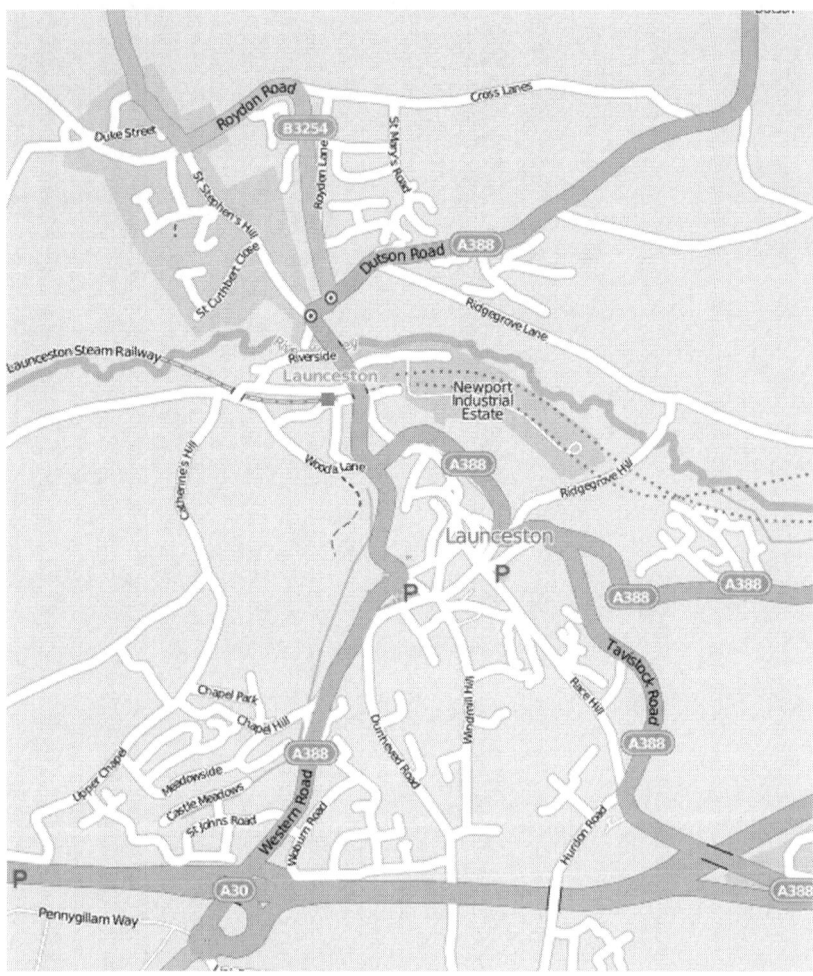

Launceston © OpenStreetMap contributors

Tamar Valley: Calstock, Saltash, Callington and Launceston

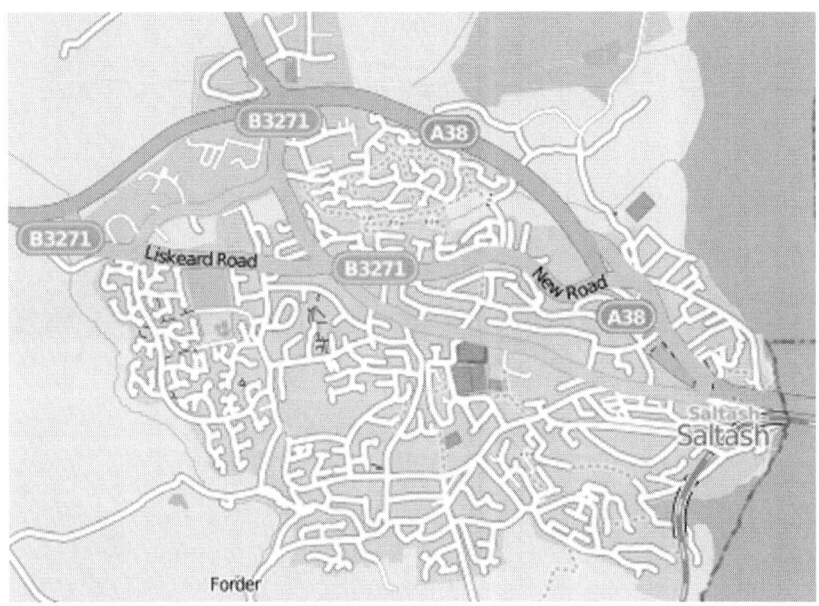

Saltash © OpenStreetMap contributors

OUR FAVOURITES

Primrose Cottage, Launceston (PL15 9PE) B & B

Primrose Cottage is set in gardens and woodlands leading down to the River Tamar. Primrose Cottage offers unique accommodation of three luxury suites with wonderful views of the Tamar Valley. Each suite has its own private entrance, sitting room, and ensuite facilities. The suites have been furnished with designer fabrics, antiques and thoughtful extra touches to provide every luxury for the visitor. Primrose Cottage is situated on the Cornwall/Devon border (4 miles from Launceston and 9 miles from Tavistock) and is well placed for exploring the North and South coasts, Dartmoor and Bodmin Moor.

Lawhitton, **Launceston**, PL15 9PE
01566 773645
http://www.primrosecottagesuites.co.uk

Tamar Valley: Calstock, Saltash, Callington and Launceston

BED & BREAKFAST

Interesting and highly rated B&Bs with a focus on your comfort and a warm welcome.

Hurdon Farm B & B
Launceston, PL15 9LS
01566 772955
http://hurdonfarm.weebly.com/
Traditional Bed and Breakfast at its best.

Primrose Cottage B & B
Lawhitton, **Launceston**, PL15 9PE
01566 773645
http://www.primrosecottagesuites.co.uk
Luxury bed and breakfast accommodation.

Trevadlock Manor & Cottages B & B
Lewannick, **Launceston**, PL15 7PW
01566 782227
http://trevadlockmanor.co.uk/
Very luxurious self-catering holiday accommodation.

Hornacott B & B
South Petherwin, **Launceston**, PL15 7LH
01566 782461
http://www.hornacott.co.uk
Hornacott is a traditional 18'th century Cornish house set in two acres of garden in the depths of the Cornish countryside.

Cullacott ★☆☆☆☆ B & B
Launceston, PL15 8NH

http://www.cullacottholidays.co.uk/
Award winning self-catering holiday cottages in North Cornwall with a unique historic twist

Erth Barton B & B
Saltash, PL12 4QY
01752 842127
http://www.erthbarton.co.uk/
Luxury B&B.

Lantallack Farm B & B
Landrake, **Saltash**, PL12 5AE
01752 851281
http://www.lantallack.co.uk

CHURCHES

These churches all have something special and are worthy of a visit. Star ratings are from Simon Jenkin's Best Churches.

St Nonna ★★★☆☆ CHURCH
Altarnun, **Launceston**, PL15 7RF

St Clederus ★☆☆☆☆ CHURCH
St Clether, **Launceston**, PL15 8PP

St Mary ★★★★☆ CHURCH
Launceston, PL15 9HA

HOUSES & CASTLES

Launceston Castle ★☆☆☆☆ HOUSE
Launceston, PL15 7DR
01566 772365
http://www.english-heritage.org.uk/daysout/properties/launceston-castle/
Set on a large natural mound, Launceston Castle dominates the surrounding landscape. Begun soon after the Norman Conquest, its focus is an unusual keep consisting of a 13th century round tower built by Richard, Earl of Cornwall, inside an earlier circular shell-keep. The tower top is now reached via a dark internal staircase.

Cotehele ★★★☆☆ HOUSE
St Dominick, **Saltash**, PL12 6TA
01579 351346
www.nationaltrust.org.uk/cotehele/
Tudor house with superb collections of textiles, armour and furniture

GARDENS

Gardens listed here have been rated by the "Good Gardens Guide".

Cotehele ★☆☆☆☆ GARDEN
St Dominick, **Saltash**, PL12 6TA
01579 351346
http://www.nationaltrust.org.uk/cotehele/
Outside, explore the formally planted terraces, or lose yourself in the Valley Garden, which includes a medieval stewpond and dovecote. Seek tranquillity in the Upper Garden or visit the two orchards planted with local apples and cherries. Cotehele Quay is the home of the restored Tamar sailing barge 'Shamrock' and gateway to a wider estate. The Discovery Centre tells the story of the Tamar Valley.

Ince Castle Gardens GARDEN
Elm Gate, **Saltash**, PL12 4QZ
01752 842672
http://www.incecastle.co.uk/
Ince Castle is at the end of a very attractive peninsula sticking out into the River Lynher opposite Antony House and gardens. The house is approached up a straight tunnel-like drive lined with daffodils which are then followed by clouds of cow parsley. The gardens, which have been planted since 1960, comprise woodland with camellias, magnolias etc and masses of bulbs and hellebores in early spring and more formal mixed beds and borders near the house, also an orchard with more bulbs and shrubs.

VIEWPOINTS

Kit Hill VIEWPOINT
Callington, PL17 8HR

Kit Hill dominates the area between Callington and the River Tamar. The word 'Kit' comes from Old English for Kite, a reference to birds of prey. Buzzards and Sparrowhawks can still be seen on the hill.

FAMILY FUN

Launceston Steam Railway FAMILY FUN
Launceston, PL15 8DA
01566 775665
http://www.launcestonsr.co.uk

Trethorne Leisure Farm FAMILY FUN
Kennards House, **Launceston**, PL15 8QE
01566 86324
http://www.trethorneleisure.com
Children will be entertained for hours in our large indoor and out door play areas, as well as a programme of animal activities throughout the day. Features Ten-Pin Bowling, Dodgems and a Games Arcade.

Jamaica Inn Museum FAMILY FUN
Bolventor, **Launceston**, PL15 7TS
01566 86250
http://www.jamaicainn.co.uk
Enter into the evil yet romantic era of smuggling in Cornwall and see what is probably the finest collection of smuggling artefacts in the country. Smuggling evolved when customs dues were first introduced in the thirteenth century but there was no form of law and order until the fifteenth century and even then it was negligible. Goods such as silks, tea, tobacco and brandy were more frequently smuggled into Cornwall than anywhere else in England.

Tamar Otter Park FAMILY FUN
North Petherwin, **North Petherwin**, PL15 8GW
01566 785646

GOLF COURSES

Courses in this guide have reached a very good standard and have something special to offer the advanced and novice player alike.

Launceston Golf Club ★★☆☆☆ GOLF

St Stephens, **Launceston**, PL15 8HF
01566 773442
www.launcestongolfclub.co.uk/
Launceston Golf Club is a friendly members club and a great venue for a days golf.

St Mellion Hotel Golf & Country Club ★★★★☆ GOLF

St Mellion, **Saltash**, PL12 6SD
01579 351351
www.st-mellion.co.uk/

China Fleet Country Club ★★★☆☆ GOLF

Saltash, PL12 6LJ
01752 854658
www.china-fleet.co.uk/
Located amidst the sweeping Cornish countryside, China Fleet is widely known for its second-to-none golfing facilities. Whatever your age or ability, and whatever the weather, we have something to suit all golfers.

ANTIQUES

Antique Chairs & Museum ANTIQUES
Colhay Farm, Polson, **Launceston**, PL15 9QS
01566 777485
http://www.antiquechairs.biz

North East Cornwall: Boscastle, Bude, Padstow, Port Isaac, Rock, Wade

A wildly beautiful landscape, the north east Atlantic coast is dotted with pretty towns and villages. A world-renowned hub for surfers and thrill-seekers, you'll find celebrity eateries, top class accommodation and spectacular coastline.

Morwenstow This tiny place in the extreme NE corner of Cornwall boasts the most eccentric vicar of the 19th century –RS Hawker who has a hut here on the cliff edge where he would sit, covered in seaweed looking out for wrecks when he would give the survivors a church yard burial rather than the normal practice of beach burial. He invented the Harvest Festival and wrote the Cornish Anthem – Trelawny. The Bush is a particularly delightful pub.

Boscastle is the only significant harbour for 20 miles, it is dramatically narrow behind its walls built in 1584 and still remembered for a horrific flood in 2004. The visitor centre is a good introduction to the local coastal scene and the Museum of Witchcraft and the Tamar Otter & Wildlife Centre are both popular. At the top of this steep village is a pub called *Napoleon* with great views as you approach and interesting Napoleonic prints –good food and beer.

Tintagel is but a few miles SW of Boscastle and is one of the most visited sites in Britain. Birthplace of the legendary King Arthur, and the scene of the story of Tristan & Isolde – it has a certain magic that is not all 'Rexque quondam futurus (the once and future king)' *Tintagel Post Office*(NT) is a rare example of a really ancient house, 14th century.

Bude, with stupendous beaches north and south it is the most accessible surfing mecca in the county. It has the only carboniferous limestone cliffs in Cornwall with jagged rocks about their base – rocks that have claimed record numbers of shipwrecks.

Crackington Haven is a small unspoilt cove favoured by geology students, amongst others, because of the visible folded sedimentary rock formations. Just a mile south is High Cliff – at 735 feet it is Cornwall's highest and southern Britain's highest sheer-drop cliff.

Padstow is a bustling harbour made famous by Rick Stein. The gastronomic revolution he inspired helped make the whole area a focus for upscale second homes. Here the mouth of the River Camel is partially protected by the Doom Bar (sand bank) though most people think it's a pint of ale. It is also the start and end point for the Camel Trail.

At 20 minute intervals a passenger ferry connects **Padstow** and **Rock** where the Restaurant Nathan Outlaw 'does awe-inspiring food from a top talent'. This is from the Good Food Guide which rates it at 9 out of 10 cooking points, the only such west of Berkshire. It also has two Michelin stars, dinner only – set menu £85 – an experience. May Day in Padstow is one of those events for which Cornwall is renowned – the 'obby oss' or simply the 'oss', now two of them, are at the centre of a festival that lasts all day. The accordion bands play, there is much singing and shouting to persuade the 'oss' out of its house and much pushing it around – all great fun. Helston and Penzance also have these uniquely Cornish celebrations. It all has a slightly pagan and south European feel.

Hawkers Cove near Padstow

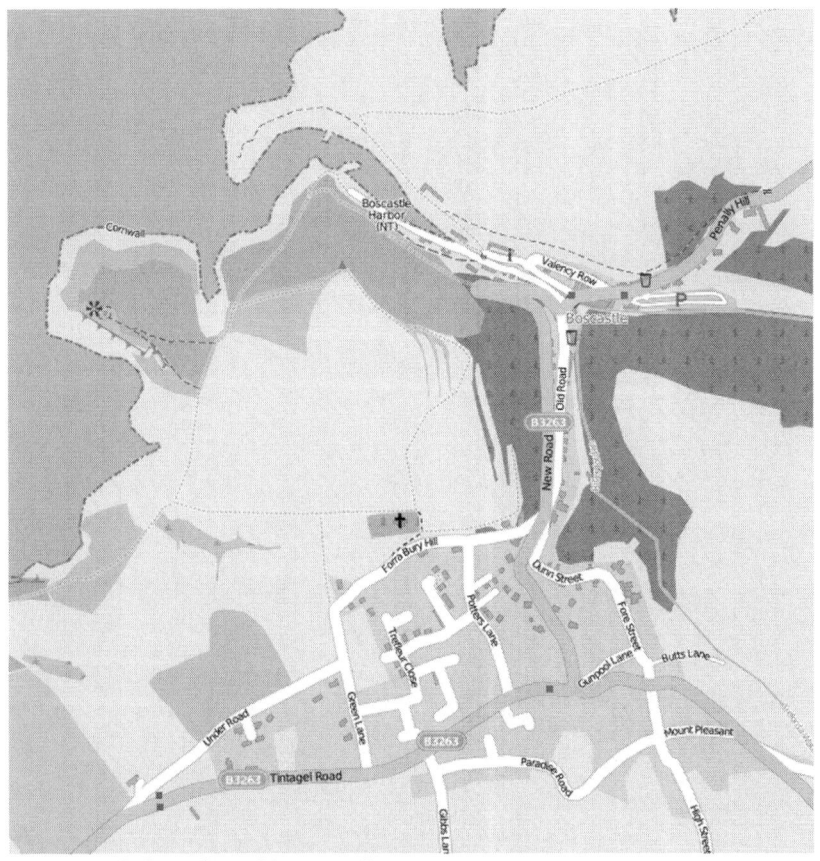

North East Cornwall: Boscastle, Bude, Padstow, Port Isaac, Rock, Wade

Boscastle © OpenStreetMap contributors

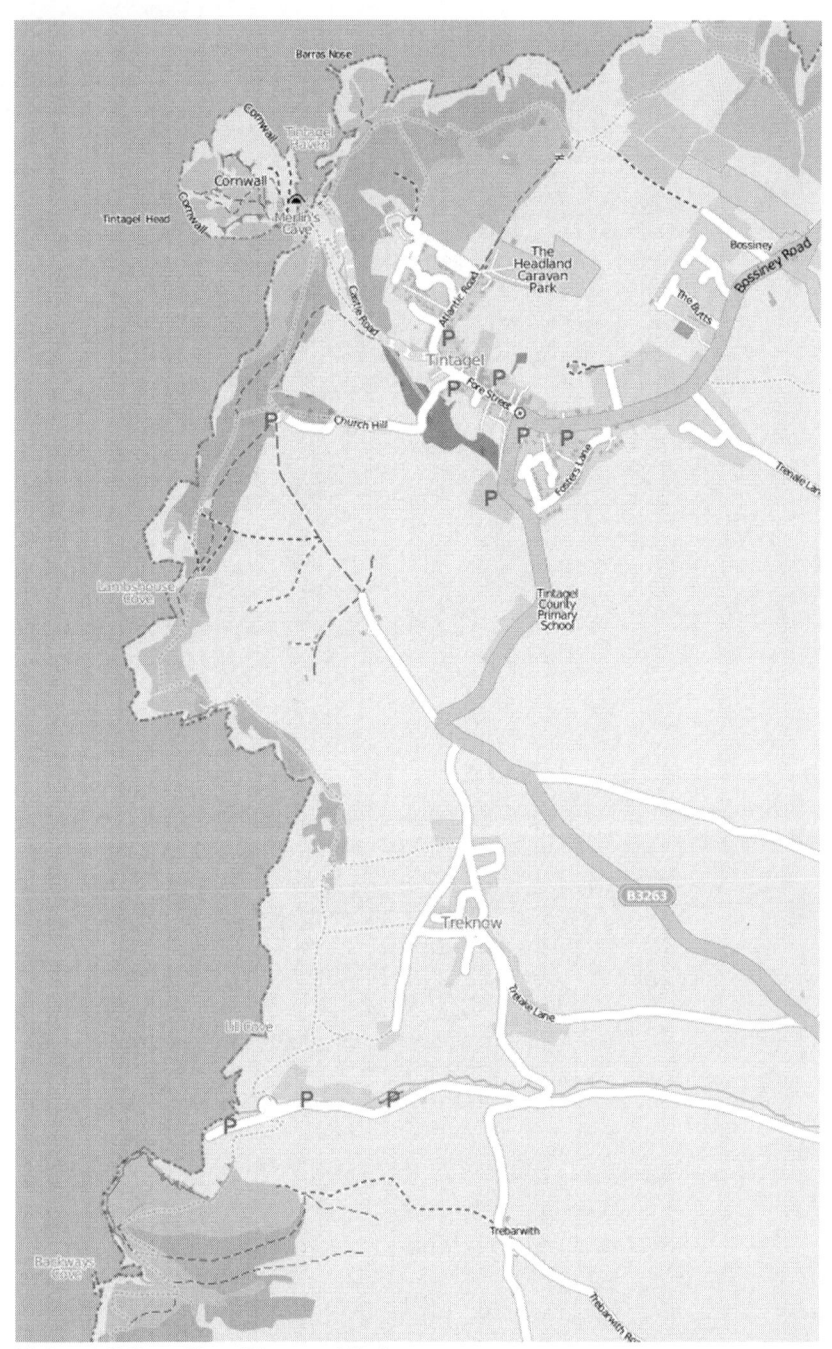

North East Cornwall: Boscastle, Bude, Padstow, Port Isaac, Rock, Wade

Tintagel © OpenStreetMap contributors

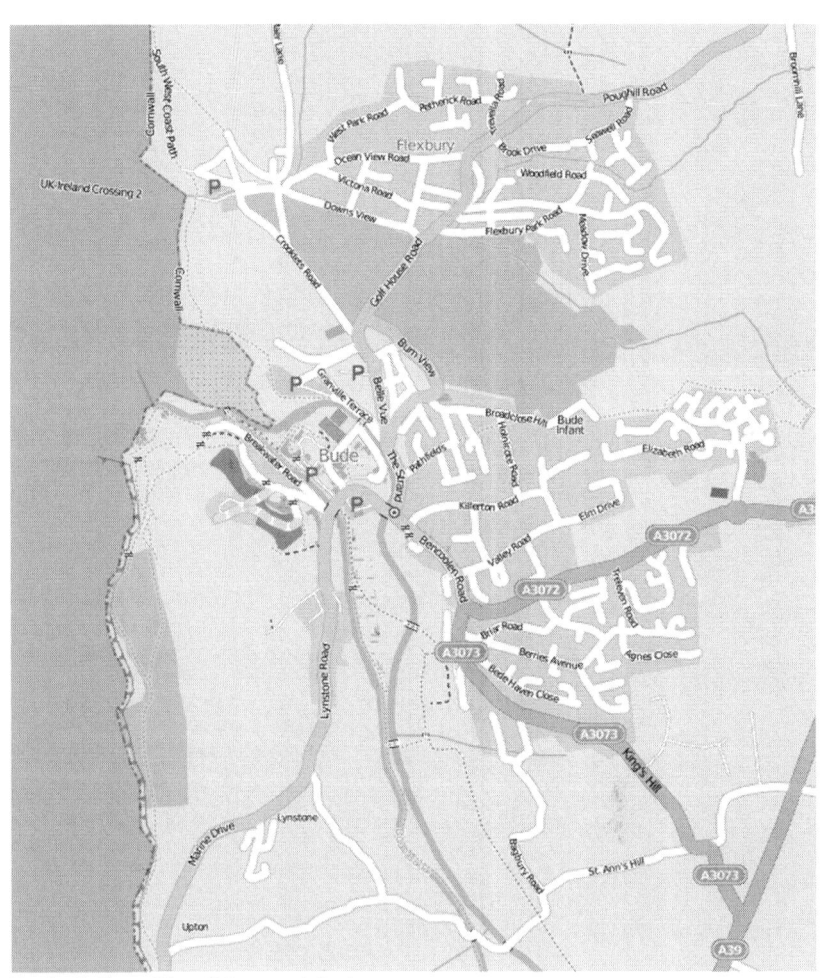

North East Cornwall: Boscastle, Bude, Padstow, Port Isaac, Rock, Wade

Bude © OpenStreetMap contributors

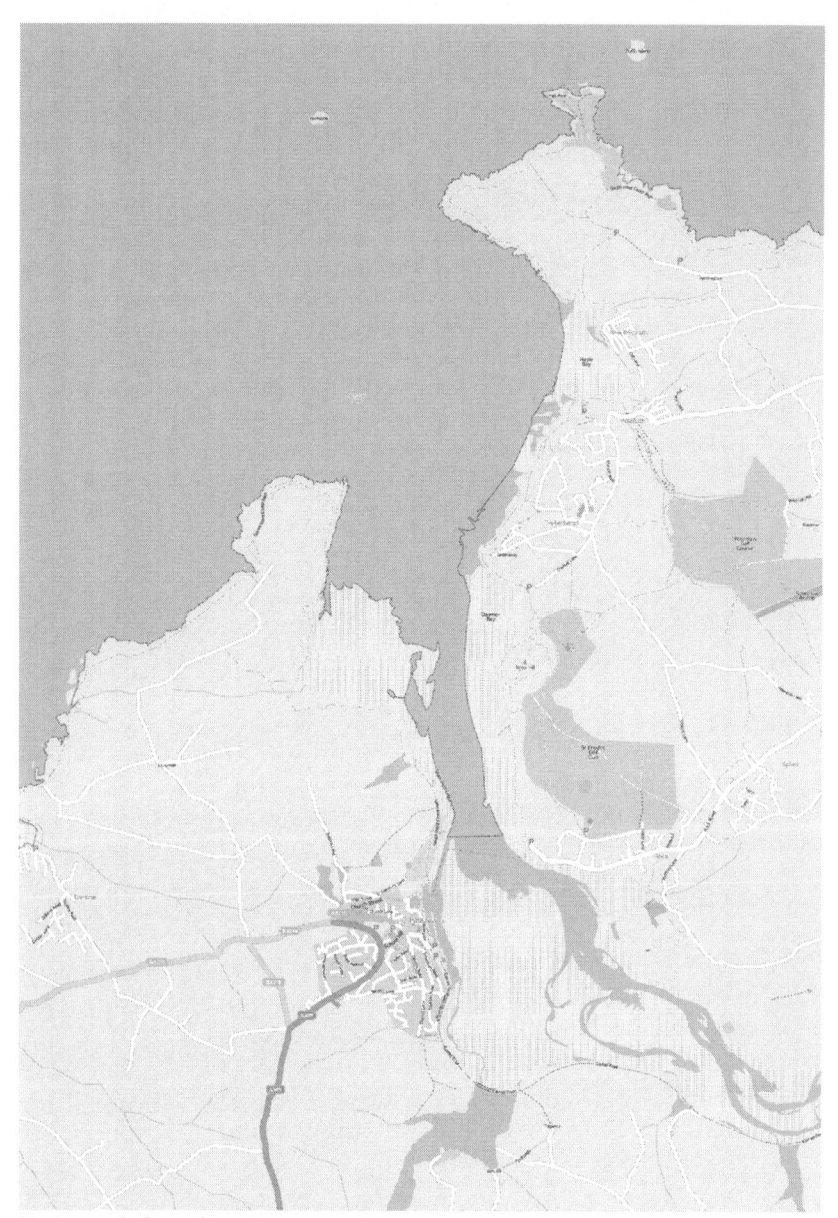

North East Cornwall: Boscastle, Bude, Padstow, Port Isaac, Rock, Wade

Padstow © OpenStreetMap contributors

North East Cornwall: Boscastle, Bude, Padstow, Port Isaac, Rock, Wade

OUR FAVOURITES

Victoria Antiques, Wadebridge (PL27 7DD)
ANTIQUES

The largest independent antique shop in Cornwall and most of the west country, having a large cross section of georgian victorian and edwardian furniture, clocks, barometers and painted furniture with one whole floor of chairs.

21 Molesworth Street, **Wadebridge**, PL27 7DD
01208 814160
http://www.vicantiques.co.uk/

North East Cornwall: Boscastle, Bude, Padstow, Port Isaac, Rock, Wade

HOTELS

A selection of superior hotels, big or small, where you can be assured of quality, comfort and a warm welcome.

The Bottreaux HOTEL
Boscastle, PL35 0BG
01840 250231
http://www.boscastlecornwall.co.uk

Trerosewill Farmhouse HOTEL
Boscastle, PL35 0BL
01840 250545
http://www.trerosewill.co.uk

The Old Rectory HOTEL
St Juliot, Nr Boscastle, **Boscastle**, PL35 0BT
01840 250225
http://www.stjuliot.com

The Beach at Bude HOTEL
Summerleaze Crescent, **Bude**, EX23 8HL
01288 389800
http://www.thebeachatbude.co.uk

Treglos Hotel HOTEL
Constantine Bay, **Padstow**, PL28 8JH
01841 520727
http://www.tregloshotel.com/

Seafood Restaurant HOTEL
Riverside, **Padstow**, PL28 8BY
01841 532700
http://www.rickstein.com

Port Gaverne Hotel HOTEL
Near Port Issac, **Port Isaac**, PL29 3SQ
01208 880244
http://www.port-gaverne-hotel.co.uk

St Enodoc Hotel HOTEL
Wadebridge, **Rock**, PL27 6LA
01208 863394
http://www.enodoc-hotel.co.uk

St Moritz Hotel HOTEL
Trebetherick, **Wadebridge**, PL27 6SD
01208 862242
http://www.stmoritzhotel.co.uk

The Hotel & Extreme Academy HOTEL
On the Beach, **Watergate Bay**, TR8 4AA
01637 860543
http://www.watergatebay.co.uk/

North East Cornwall: Boscastle, Bude, Padstow, Port Isaac, Rock, Wade

BED & BREAKFAST

Interesting and highly rated B&Bs with a focus on your comfort and a warm welcome.

Trewardale B & B
Blisland, **Bodmin**, PL30 4HS
01208 821226
http://www.trewardale.com/
A beautiful grade II* listed Georgian Manor on the edge of Bodmin Moor surrounded by its own private gardens and rolling farmland.

Reddivallen Farm B & B
Trevalga, **Boscastle**, PL35 0EE
01840 250854
http://www.redboscastle.com/
Reddivallen is tucked away in a secluded location offering the tranquil of the countryside.

Sudcott Park B & B
Jacobstow, **Bude**, EX22 6XR
01288 341155
http://www.sudcottpark.co.uk
Stunning views in an idyllic setting.

Trevigue B & B
Crackington Haven, **Bude**, EX23 0LQ
01840 230492
http://www.trevigue.co.uk
A warm Cornish welcome and fresh local food.

Upton Lodge B & B
Bude, EX23 0LY
01288 354126

Higher Trewint Farmhouse B & B
Poundstock, **Bude**, EX23 0EQ
01840 230 342
http://www.highertrewintbandb.co.uk
Higher Trewint is a Victorian farmhouse set on a farm in an area of outstanding natural beauty with panoramic views of the North Cornwall and Devon coast.

Creathorne Farm B & B
Widemouth Bay, **Bude**, EX23 0NE
01288 316077
http://www.creathornefarm.co.uk
Luxury self-catering accommodation.

Molesworth Manor B & B
Little Petherick, **Padstow**, PL27 7QT
01841 540292
http://www.molesworthmanor.co.uk/

Ballaminers House B & B
Little Petherick, **Padstow**, PL27 7QT
01841 540933
http://www.ballaminershouse.co.uk
Luxury self-catering cornish stone farmhouse.

Mother Ivey Cottage B & B
Trevose Head, **Padstow**, PL28 8SL
01841 520329
http://www.trevosehead.co.uk/

North East Cornwall: Boscastle, Bude, Padstow, Port Isaac, Rock, Wade

Caradoc of Tregardock B & B
Treligga, Delabole, **Port Isaac**, PL33 9ED
01840 213300
http://www.tregardock.com
Luxury accommodation in North Cornwall.

Tregellist Farm B & B
Tregellist, **St Kew**, PL30 3HG
01208 880537
http://www.tregellistfarm.co.uk/
Lovely walks are to be found everywhere in this area, both open country and coastal.

Treliver Farm B & B
St Wenn, **St Tudy**, PL30 5PQ
01726 890286
http://www.treliverfarm.co.uk

Polrode Mill B & B
Cottage Allen Valley, **St Tudy**, PL30 3NS
01208 850203
http://www.polrodeguesthouse.co.uk/
17th Century Country Guest House in the heart of north Cornwall.

Porteath Barn B & B
St Minver, **Wadebridge**, PL27 6RA
01208 863605
Luxurious B&B.

Roskear B & B
St Breock, **Wadebridge**, PL27 7HU
01208 812805
http://www.roskear.com
High Quality Bed and Breakfast in a 18th Century Farmhouse

Grogley Farm B & B
Wadebridge, PL30 5NP
01637 881942

An 18th century Cornish stone and slate farmhouse, set in its own private gardens near the charming hamlet of Ruthernbridge.

PUBS/GASTROPUBS

Above average pubs serving quality real ale, excellent bar food or both.

The Cobweb Inn `PUB`
The Bridge, **Boscastle**, PL35 0HE
01840 250278
http://www.cobwebinn.co.uk/
Traditional Cornish Public House.

Bush `PUB`
Morwenstow, EX23 9SR
01288 331242
http://www.bushinn-morwenstow.co.uk
The Bush Inn at Morwenstow is a 13th century free house in a stunning location.

The Port Gaverne Hotel `PUB`
Port Issac, PL29 3SQ
01208 880244
http://www.port-gaverne-hotel.co.uk/
A 17th century restored inn that is full of charm and steeped in history. Offers a bar and restaurant menu.

The Cornish Arms `GASTRO PUB`
Churchtown, St Merryn, **Padstow**, PL28 8ND
01841 532700
http://www.rickstein.com/The-Cornish-Arms.html
A simple British pub menu with a Rick Stein twist.

North East Cornwall: Boscastle, Bude, Padstow, Port Isaac, Rock, Wade

RESTAURANTS

Only top notch restaurants are listed here. Cooking stars are drawn from "The Good Food Guide 2013".

Rojano's in the Square ★★☆☆☆☆☆☆☆☆
RESTAURANT

9 Mill Square, **Padstow**, PL28 8AE
01841 532796
www.rojanos.co.uk
Italian by Paul Ainsworth.

The Seafood Restaurant ★★★☆☆☆☆☆☆☆
RESTAURANT

Riverside, **Padstow**, PL28 8BY
01841 532700
http://www.rickstein.com
Where 'Padstein' brand was born & still going strong.

St Petroc's Bistro ★☆☆☆☆☆☆☆☆☆ **RESTAURANT**

4 New Street, **Padstow**, PL28 8EA
01841 532700
http://www.rickstein.com

Rick Stein's Café ★☆☆☆☆☆☆☆☆☆ **RESTAURANT**

10 Middle Street, **Padstow**, PL28 8BQ
01841 532700
http://www.rickstein.com
Throbbing informal café.

Paul Ainsworth at No.6 ★★★★★☆☆☆☆
RESTAURANT

6 Middle Street, **Padstow**, PL28 8AP
01841 532093
http://www.number6inpadstow.co.uk
Awarded first Michelin star in 2013. Serving local, seasonal ingredients served in a simple modern style with a Cornish and British influence.

Restaurant Nathan Outlaw ★★★★★★★★★☆
RESTAURANT

St Enodoc Hotel, Rock Road, **Rock**, PL27 6LA
12208 863394
http://www.nathan-outlaw.com
2 Michelin stars. Nothing to match it in the West.

Nathan Outlaw Seafood & Grill ★★★★☆☆☆☆☆☆
RESTAURANT

St Enodoc Hotel, Rock Road, **Rock**, PL27 6LA
01208 863394
http://www.nathan-outlaw.com
Brasserie style, simple quality cooking.

Fifteen ★★★☆☆☆☆☆☆☆ RESTAURANT

On the beach, **Watergate Bay**, TR8 4AA
01637 861000
http://www.fifteencornwall.co.uk
Fab on a glorious beach

North East Cornwall: Boscastle, Bude, Padstow, Port Isaac, Rock, Wade

CHURCHES

These churches all have something special and are worthy of a visit. Star ratings are from Simon Jenkin's Best Churches.

St James ★☆☆☆☆ CHURCH
Kilkhampton, **Bude**, EX23 9QZ

St Swithin ★★★☆☆ CHURCH
W of Bude, **Launcells**, EX23 9NQ

St John the Baptist ★★☆☆☆ CHURCH
Northernmost point, **Morwenstow**, EX23 9SR

St Endelienta ★★☆☆☆ CHURCH
B3314 E of Padstow, **St Endellion**, PL29 3TP

St Materiana ★★★☆☆ CHURCH
N Coast, **Tintagel**, PL34 0DD

St Enodoc's Church ★☆☆☆☆ CHURCH
Trebetherick, PL27 6SG
John Betjeman is buried here.

North East Cornwall: Boscastle, Bude, Padstow, Port Isaac, Rock, Wade

HOUSES & CASTLES

Prideaux Place ★★★☆☆ HOUSE
Padstow, PL28 8RP
01841 532411
www.prideauxplace.co.uk/
This stunningly beautiful Elizabethan manor house overlooks the picturesque fishing harbour of Padstow in North Cornwall.

Tintagel Old Post Office ★★☆☆☆ HOUSE
Fore Street, **Tintagel**, PL34 0DB
01840 770024
www.nationaltrust.org.uk/tintagel-old-post-office/
Tintagel Old Post Office is a 14th-century stone house, built to the plan of a medieval manor house.

BEACHES

All of our beaches have the stamp of approval from the Marine Conservation Society (http://www.mcsuk.org/).

Crackington Haven BEACH
Boscastle, EX23 8NF
Shingle lifeguarded

Sandymouth BEACH
Bude, EX23 9HP
2 km sand lifeguarded

Crooklets BEACH
Bude, EX23 8NF

Sand lifeguarded

Widemouth Sand BEACH
Bude, EX23 0AW
Sand & rock pools lifegudarded

Summerleaze BEACH
Bude, EX23 8LG

Sand lifeguarded

Rock BEACH
Padstow, PL27
Sand

Treyarmon Bay BEACH
Padstow, PL28 8JN
Sand sheltered lifeguarded

Porthcothan BEACH
Padstow, PL28 8LN
Sand lifeguarded

Constantine Bay BEACH
Padstow, PL28 8JJ
Sand lifeguarded

Daymer Beach BEACH
Padstow, PL27 6SA
Sand

Harlyn Bay BEACH
Padstow, PL28 8EX
Sand surfing lifeguarded

Mother Ivey's Bay BEACH
Padstow, PL28 8SL
Sand

Trebarwith Strand BEACH
Tintagel, PL34 0HB
Sand lifeguarded

Polzeath BEACH
Wadebridge, PL27 6SP
Sand shingle lifeguarded

VIEWPOINTS

Carnewas and Bedruthan Steps VIEWPOINT
Padstow, PL27 7UW

http://www.nationaltrust.org.uk/carnewas-and-bedruthan-steps/
Dramatic coastline with views over huge rock stacks

North East Cornwall: Boscastle, Bude, Padstow, Port Isaac, Rock, Wade

FAMILY FUN

King Arthur's Great Halls FAMILY FUN
Sound & Light show - Tintagel, **Tintagel**, PL34 0AD
01840 770526
http://www.kingarthursgreathalls.com

Tintagel Castle FAMILY FUN
Bossiney Road, **Tintagel**, PL34 0HE
01840 770328
www.tintagelcastle.co.uk/
Tintagel Castle stands on windswept cliffs in North Cornwall on one of England's most dramatic coastlines. The Castle is believed to be the birthplace of King Arthur who, as legend has it, was protected from the evil magician Merlin by his magical sword, Excaliber.

Crealy Great Adventure Park FAMILY FUN
Tredinnick, **Wadebridge**, PL27 7RA
01841 540276
http://www.crealy.co.uk
Large indoor adventure zone.

NATURAL PRODUCE

Whalesborough Farm Foods
NATURAL PRODUCE

Marhamchurch, Bude, **Bude**, EX23 0SD
01288 361317
http://seproudfoot@aol.com
Award wining cheeses - various

Chough Bakery NATURAL PRODUCE
3 The Strand, Padstow, **Padstow**, PL28 8AJ
01841 532835
http://www.thechoughbakery.co.uk
Pasties & designer breads

North East Cornwall: Boscastle, Bude, Padstow, Port Isaac, Rock, Wade

GOLF COURSES

Courses in this guide have reached a very good standard and have something special to offer the advanced and novice player alike.

Bude & North Cornwall Golf Club ★★★★☆ GOLF
Burn View, **Bude**, EX23 8DA
01288 352006
www.budegolf.co.uk/
Bude & North Cornwall Golf Club, surrounded by the town and the sea, is a challenging 18 hole links course established in 1891.

Trevose Golf & Country Club ★★★★☆ GOLF
Constantine Bay, **Padstow**, PL28 8JB
01841 520208
www.trevose-gc.co.uk/
Trevose offers three courses, catering for golfers of all standards - from complete novices to seasoned golfers and touring professionals. The "Championship Course" ranks as one of the top links golf courses in the British Isles. The "Headland Course" is the ideal 9 hole alternative to The Championship Course with a challenging layout and fast greens. The "Short Course" is ideal for beginners, juniors and those more accomplished golfers looking to refine their short game.

The Point at Polzeath ★★★☆☆ GOLF
St Minver, **Polzeath**, PL27 6QT
01208 863000
http://www.thepointatpolzeath.co.uk/
Set in the hills just above Polzeath on the North Cornish Coast, the 18 hole golf course and 12 bay covered driving range is surrounded by beautiful countryside and has spectacular views towards the sea.

St Enodoc Golf Club ★★★★☆ GOLF

Rock, **Wadebridge**, PL27 6LD
01208 863216
www.st-enodoc.co.uk/
St Enodoc Golf Club on the North Cornwall coast overlooks the Camel Estuary, with Padstow on the far side, and to the North out across the Atlantic. The location on the high sand dunes is ideal for golf combined with stunning sea views.

North East Cornwall: Boscastle, Bude, Padstow, Port Isaac, Rock, Wade

ANTIQUES

Victoria Antiques ANTIQUES
21 Molesworth Street, **Wadebridge**, PL27 7DD
01208 814160
http://www.vicantiques.co.uk/
Georgian, Edwardian and Victorian furniture.

North West Cornwall: Newquay, Mawgan Porth, Perranporth, St Agnes, Watergate Bay

Again the rugged beauty of the Atlantic coastline and the picturesque towns and villages make this an excellent holiday location for families and thrill-seekers alike.

Newquay Because of its unsurpassed beaches, it is the foremost surfing centre not just of Cornwall but of Britain. It has a railway station which is the only branch line in Britain to have scheduled InterCity services from May to September. During this period the population can grow from its normal 20,000 to about 100,000.
This busy harbour town has a laid back atmosphere but the formerly tacky facilities are giving way to the requirements of the more moneyed classes that enjoy its unique sporting facilities, like the *Extreme Academy* to Kite surf, Traction kite, Wave ski, Stand-up paddle surf, Hand planing. Jamie Oliver's *Fifteen Cornwall* at Watergate Bay is a terrific place, right on with kids, spectacular views, very good food and funky wine list.

Trerice (NT) is a 16th century house 3 miles from Newquay. It has the most famous plasterwork in Cornwall. Though not a big house it really is a charming place and a change of gear from the Newquay scene.

Mawgan Porth, Perranporth, Watergate Bay – all famous beaches – see beaches

St Agnes From the 17th to the early 20th centuries this was an important centre for mining, arsenic, tin and copper (the two ingredients of bronze) and so is of great interest to industrial archaeologists. It is a town of some charm with the ruin s of the fourth harbour to be built here. All were destroyed by storms but the last one lasted throughout the 19th century allowing direct export from the mines.

North West Cornwall: Newquay, Mawgan Porth, Perranporth, St Agnes, Watergate Bay

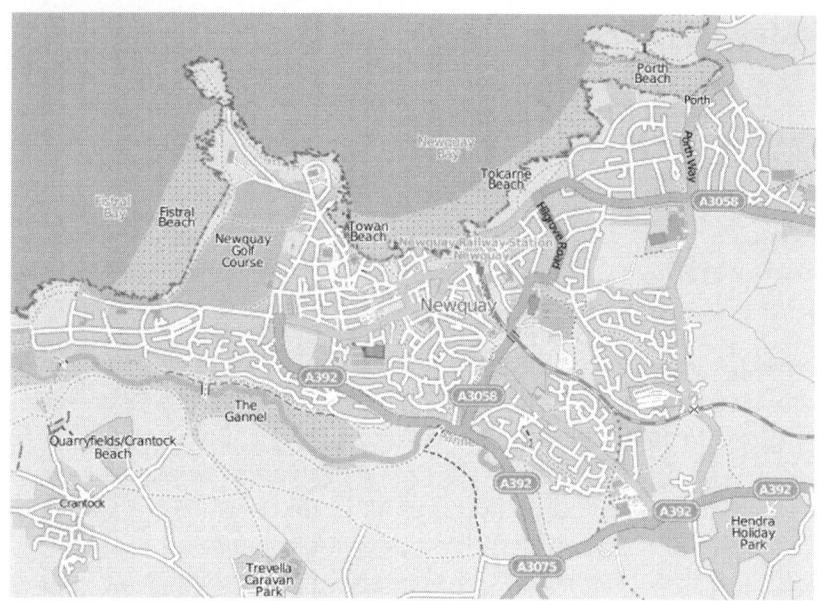

Newquay © OpenStreetMap contributors

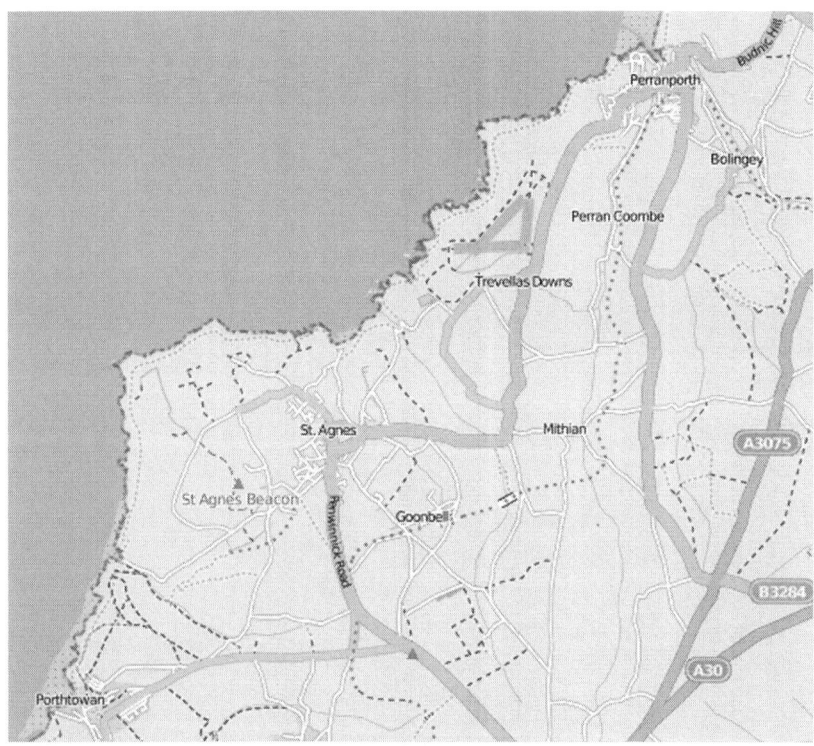

North West Cornwall: Newquay, Mawgan Porth, Perranporth, St Agnes, Watergate Bay

St Agnes & Perranporth © OpenStreetMap contributors

North West Cornwall: Newquay, Mawgan Porth, Perranporth, St Agnes, Watergate Bay

HOTELS

A selection of superior hotels, big or small, where you can be assured of quality, comfort and a warm welcome.

Bedruthan Steps Hotel HOTEL
NE of Newquay off B3276, **Mawgan Porth**, TR8 4BU
01637 860555
http://www.bedruthan.com

The Scarlet Hotel HOTEL
Tredragon Road, **Mawgan Porth**, TR8 4DQ
01637 861800
http://www.scarlethotel.co.uk

Headland Hotel HOTEL
Fistral Beach, **Newquay**, TR7 1EW
01637 872211
http://www.headlandhotel.co.uk

Rose in Vale HOTEL
Mithian, **St Agnes**, TR5 0QD
01872 552202
http://www.rose-in-vale-hotel.co.uk

North West Cornwall: Newquay, Mawgan Porth, Perranporth, St Agnes, Watergate Bay

BED & BREAKFAST

Interesting and highly rated B&Bs with a focus on your comfort and a warm welcome.

Drym Farm B & B
Camborne, TR14 0NU
01209 831039
http://www.drymfarm.co.uk
Although rural and peaceful, Drym Farm is ideally positioned between the north and south coasts, and makes a great base to tour from.

SeaScape B & B
Tregurrian, **Newquay**, TR8 4AD
01637 860838

Stunning views across the bay towards Newquay Headland - an ideal central location for touring Cornwall.

Degembris Farmhouse B & B
St Newlyn East, **Newquay**, TR8 5HY
01872 510555
http://www.degembris.co.uk
Farmhouse B&B, Self Catering cottages and Rural Retreats.

Cleaderscroft B & B
16 British Road, **St Agnes**, TR5 0TZ
01872 552349
http://www.cchotel.fsnet.co.uk
A small family owned and run hotel.

North West Cornwall: Newquay, Mawgan Porth, Perranporth, St Agnes, Watergate Bay

The Driftwood Spars B & B
Trevaunance Cove, **St Agnes**, TR5 0RT
01872 552 428
http://www.driftwoodspars.com/
Quality guest accommodation attached to a traditional Cornish pub.

Upton Farm B & B
Delabole, **Trebarwith**, PL33 9DG
01840 770225
http://www.upton-farm.co.uk
Luxury Bed & Breakfast and a choice of Self catering cottages.

North West Cornwall: Newquay, Mawgan Porth, Perranporth, St Agnes, Watergate Bay

PUBS/GASTROPUBS

Above average pubs serving quality real ale, excellent bar food or both.

Plume of Feathers PUB
Mitchell, TR8 5AX
01872 510387

Blue Bar PUB
Beach Road, East Cliff, **Porthtowan**, TR4 8AW
01209 890329
http://www.blue-bar.co.uk/
Blue is Cornwall's original beach bar & kitchen, with stunning views, an enviable location with freshly prepared great food & Barista coffees.

Driftwood Spars PUB
Trevaunance Cove, **St Agnes**, TR5 0RT
01872 552428
http://www.driftwoodspars.com/
A micro brewery for discerning ale drinkers, being rated in the top 10 pubs with rooms, real ales and real fires in the Financial Times in September 2010 and in the top five of the Times' 50 best pubs in the country 2011.

North West Cornwall: Newquay, Mawgan Porth, Perranporth, St Agnes, Watergate Bay

RESTAURANTS

Only top notch restaurants are listed here. Cooking stars are drawn from "The Good Food Guide 2013".

New Yard Restaurant ★★★★☆☆☆☆☆
RESTAURANT

Trelowarren Estate, **Mawgan Porth**, TR12 6AF
01326 221595
http://www.newyardrestaurant.co.uk/
Locally sourced, fresh, seasonal Cornish ingredients, cooked simply.

The Herring ★★★☆☆☆☆☆☆ RESTAURANT

Bedruthan Steps Hotel, **Mawgan Porth**, TR8 4BU
01637 860860
www.bedruthan.com
Vibrant new cliff-top seafood restaurant with chefs from Porthminster Beach Café.

North West Cornwall: Newquay, Mawgan Porth, Perranporth, St Agnes, Watergate Bay

HOUSES & CASTLES

Trerice House ★★★☆☆ HOUSE

Kestle Mill, **Newquay**, TR8 4PG
01637 875404
http://www.nationaltrust.org.uk/trerice/

North West Cornwall: Newquay, Mawgan Porth, Perranporth, St Agnes, Watergate Bay

BEACHES

All of our beaches have the stamp of approval from the Marine Conservation Society (http://www.mcsuk.org/).

Towan Beach BEACH
Newquay, TR7
Shingle, lifeguarded

Crantock BEACH
Newquay, TR8 5RH
Sand lifeguarded

Holywell Bay BEACH
Newquay, TR8 5PR
Sand lifeguarded

Lusty glaze BEACH
Newquay, TR7 3AA
Sand lifeguarded

Mawgan Porth BEACH
Newquay, TR8 4DJ
Sand lifeguarded

Perranporth Penhale Sands BEACH
Newquay, TR6 0DP
2 miles of sand, surfing, lifeguarded

North West Cornwall: Newquay, Mawgan Porth, Perranporth, St Agnes, Watergate Bay

Watergate Bay BEACH
Newquay, TR8 4AA
2 miles of fine sand, access to hotel, water sports, lifeguarded

Great Western Beach BEACH
Newquay, TR7
Sand lifeguarded

Tolcarne Beach BEACH
Newquay, Tr7
Sand, lifeguarded

Fistral Beach BEACH
Newquay, TR7 1PY
Sand, lifeguarded, top surfing beach

Porthtowan Beach BEACH BLUE FLAG
Porthtowan, TR4 8AD
Sand, popular, lifeguarded

Trevaunce Cove BEACH
St Agnes, TR5 0RT
Sand Rock lifeguarded

77

North West Cornwall: Newquay, Mawgan Porth, Perranporth, St Agnes, Watergate Bay

VIEWPOINTS

Gwennap Pit VIEWPOINT
Redruth, TR16 5HH

www.gwennappit.co.uk/

Gwennap Pit is an open air amphitheatre, made famous by John Wesley, the founder of Methodism. Possibly a hollow created by mining activities, it has remarkable acoustic properties.

North West Cornwall: Newquay, Mawgan Porth, Perranporth, St Agnes, Watergate Bay

FAMILY FUN

Zoo FAMILY FUN
Trenance Gardens, **Newquay**, TR7 2LZ
01637 873342
http://www.newquayzoo.org.uk

Dairyland FAMILY FUN
Famous Cornwall Family Attraction - A3508 4m SE, **Newquay**, TR8 5AA
01872 510246
http://www.dairylandfarmworld.co.uk

Blue Reef Aquarium FAMILY FUN
Towan Beach, **Newquay**, TR7 1DU
01637 872134
http://www.bluereefaquarium.co.uk

Fistral Beach FAMILY FUN
Great surfing, **Newquay**, TR7 1HS
01637 850584
http://www.fistralbeach.co.uk

Extreme Academy FAMILY FUN
Extreme sports, kite surfing & the rest. Watergate Bay, **Newquay**, TR8 4AA
01637 860543
http://www.watergatebay.co.uk

Holywell Bay Fun Park FAMILY FUN
For active children - off A3075 SW, **Newquay**, TR8 5PW
01637 830095

North West Cornwall: Newquay, Mawgan Porth, Perranporth, St Agnes, Watergate Bay

http://www.holywellbay.co.uk

World in Miniature FAMILY FUN
Goonhavern, **Perranporth**, TR4 9QE
01872 572828
http://www.miniaturapark.co.uk

Cornish Goldsmiths Treasure Park FAMILY FUN
Tolgus Mill, **Redruth**, TR16 4HN
01209 203280
http://www.treasureparks.com/
Built on the site of the Tolgus Tin Mine and set in stunning grounds, Treasure Park hosts a selection of stunning retail and jewellery shops, jewellery workshops and family and children's entertainment outlets all linked by twisting paths, quiet streams and water wheels.

North West Cornwall: Newquay, Mawgan Porth, Perranporth, St Agnes, Watergate Bay

NATURAL PRODUCE

Cornish Country Larder NATURAL PRODUCE
Creamery, Trevarrian, **Newquay**, TR8 4AH
01637 860331
http://www.cclltd.co.uk
Makers of soft cheeses

Falmouth Fishselling Co NATURAL PRODUCE
Cardrew Industrial Estate, Redruth, **Redruth**, TR15 1SS
01209 314111
http://www.falfish.com
Largest on the south coast

Primrose Herd NATURAL PRODUCE
Busveal, **Redruth**, TR16 HF
01209 821408
http://www.primroseherd.co.uk/
Award Winning pork products

81

North West Cornwall: Newquay, Mawgan Porth, Perranporth, St Agnes, Watergate Bay

GOLF COURSES

Courses in this guide have reached a very good standard and have something special to offer the advanced and novice player alike.

Newquay Golf Club ★☆☆☆☆ GOLF
Tower Road, **Newquay**, TR7 1LT
01637 874354
www.newquaygolfclub.co.uk/
Newquay Golf Club is a seaside links over looking the world famous surfers' paradise of Fistral Beach.

Perranporth Golf Club ★★★★☆ GOLF
Budnic Hill, **Perranporth**, TR6 0AB
01872 573701
www.perranporthgolfclub.co.uk/
Boasts a challenging and well-maintained championship golf course as well as breathtaking views up and down the coast.

South East Cornwall: Fowey, Looe, Lostwithiel, Rame Peninsula, Polperro and Torpoint

Fowey, pronounced Foy, is a prosperous looking town right on the mouth of the river which is a yachting haven. It is all small steep streets, brightly painted houses and charm with catering for all pockets. Daphne du Maurier's Manderley in Rebecca is in life 'Menabilly' the house of the leading family of the region, the Rashleigh's. A famous resident of Fowey was Sir Arthur Quiller-Couch, poet, writer and compiler of the Oxford Book of Verse who was the inspiration for 'Ratty' in Kenneth Graham's Wind in the Willows which appears as the Thames in the story but started in the Fowey River, when he spent time here.

Looe, is a fishing town with lots of small boats bringing in the daily catch – just as good as France. The town is cut into East & West by the river Looe cutting through steep sided hills. In the middle-ages Looe was an important port for tin, arsenic, fish and boat-building. Today, tourism is even more important than fishing but the town rewards those with the curiosity to penetrate the back streets. It is a lovely walk from West Looe to Talland Bay and Polperro.

Lostwithiel, was once a stannary town and the most important in Cornwall. It is now just a pleasant place of 2,600 people and a modest decent restaurant called Asquiths. Some of the architecture bears witness to a richer past.

Polperro, is pluperfect picturesque yet somehow erring on the right side of tweeness. The Blue Peter pub has the most salient geographic position in the town and is a clear reminder of how best to enjoy the place. It's prosperity is closely linked to smuggling from the 12th C to the Napoleonic Wars which made some things so expensive that some illicit fortunes were made. The Shell House is a charmingly eccentric house decorated with a vast collection of seashells between 1937 –

42.

The Rame Peninsula bordered by Plymouth Sound to the east and called after the cape at its tip, it contains two of Cornwall most attractive properties: Antony House is a pure 18th C mansion of dolls' house prettiness (says Simon Jenkins). Descendants of the builder still live in it though it now belongs to the NT. The southerly views are lovely and have a water sculpture by the most celebrated man in that art form – William Pye. Mount Edgcumbe is an Elizabethan house undone by the vicissitudes of the 20th C, including a bomb in the last war. Behind its sandstone façade in the style of the original is a modern house that belongs to Plymouth City Council & Cornwall Council. The Country Park of 865 acres contains a series of formal gardens but the undisputed glory is the sight of all those acres in Camellia bloom. *The Finneygook* in nearby Crafthole is very pleasant pub.

St Germans church is well worth a detour: originally Saxon but mainly Norman with a front like a cathedral. It has been much rebuilt but the atmosphere is still Norman. The east window is one of the finest works of Burne-Jones and a 1722 monument to Edward Eliot – the ancient and current leading family, is by Rysbrack and is likely the finest in Cornwall.

Torpoint is known mainly for the three ferries dating from 2005 that join Cornwall and Devon. They have had competition from the Tamar Road Bridge since it opened in 1961. It has been much enlarged since and now carries over 40, 000 vehicles a day.

Polperro Harbour

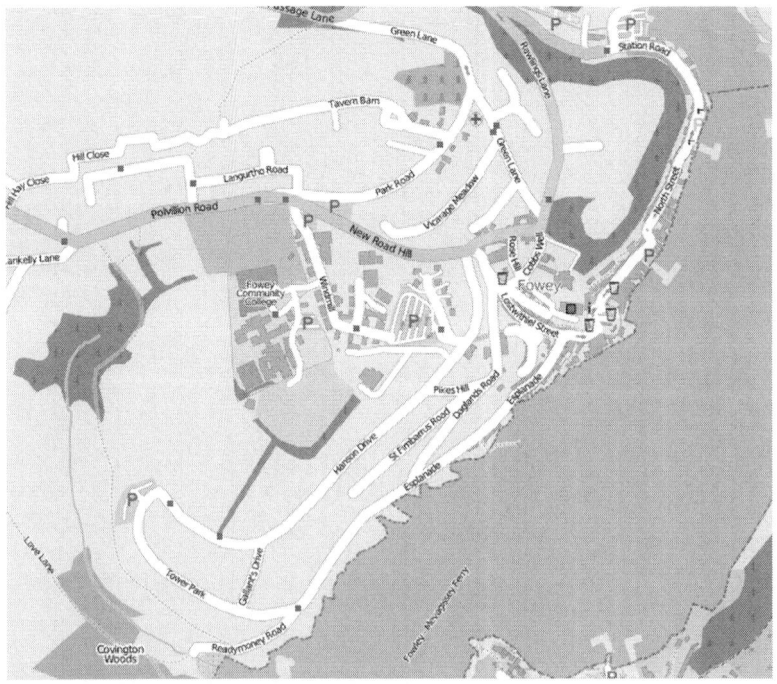

Fowey © OpenStreetMap contributors

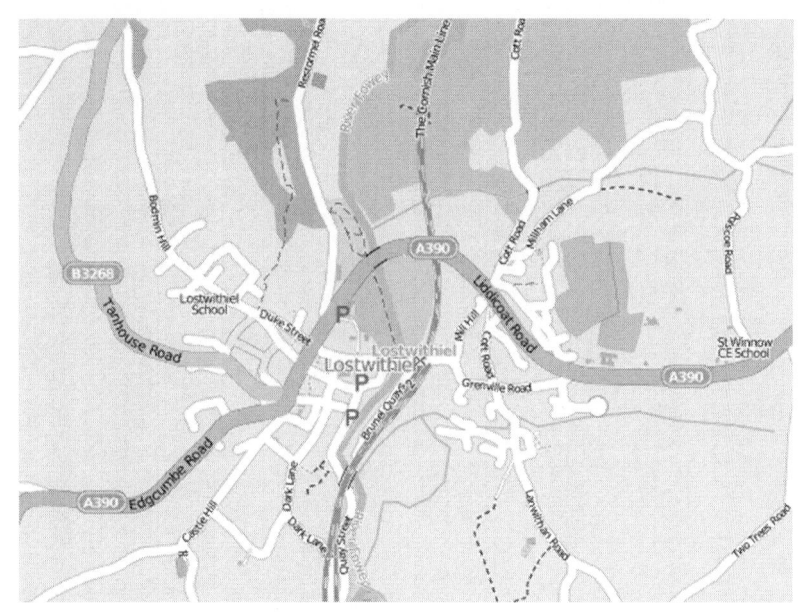

South East Cornwall: Fowey, Looe, Lostwithiel, Rame Peninsula, Polperro and Torpoint

Lostwithiel © OpenStreetMap contributors

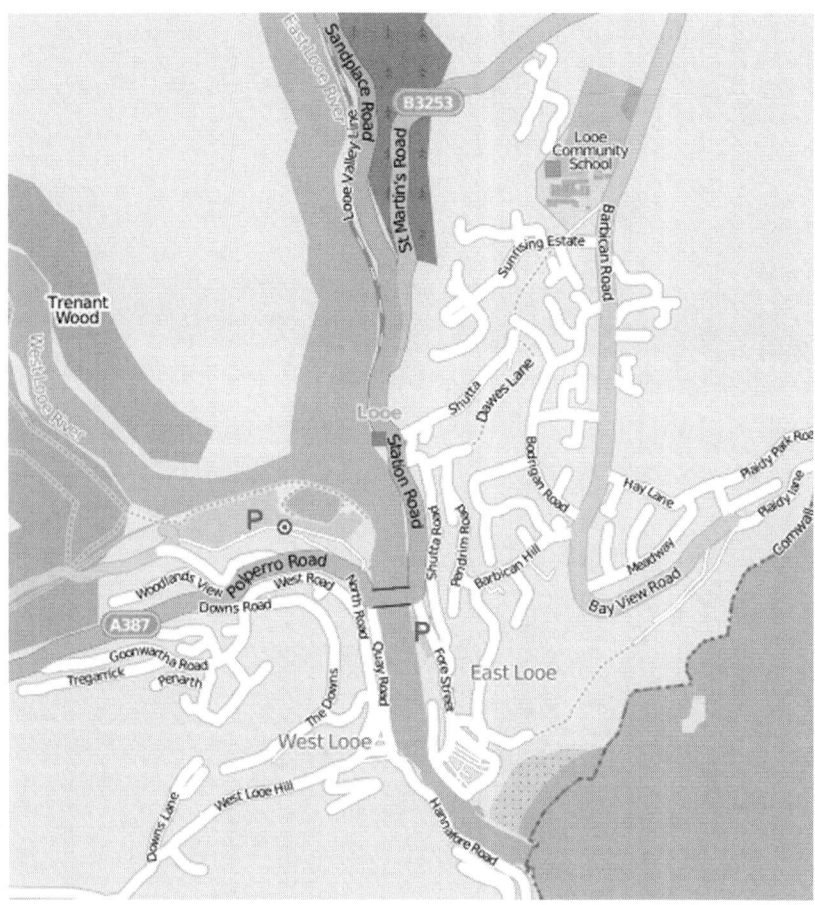

South East Cornwall: Fowey, Looe, Lostwithiel, Rame Peninsula, Polperro and Torpoint

Looe © OpenStreetMap contributors

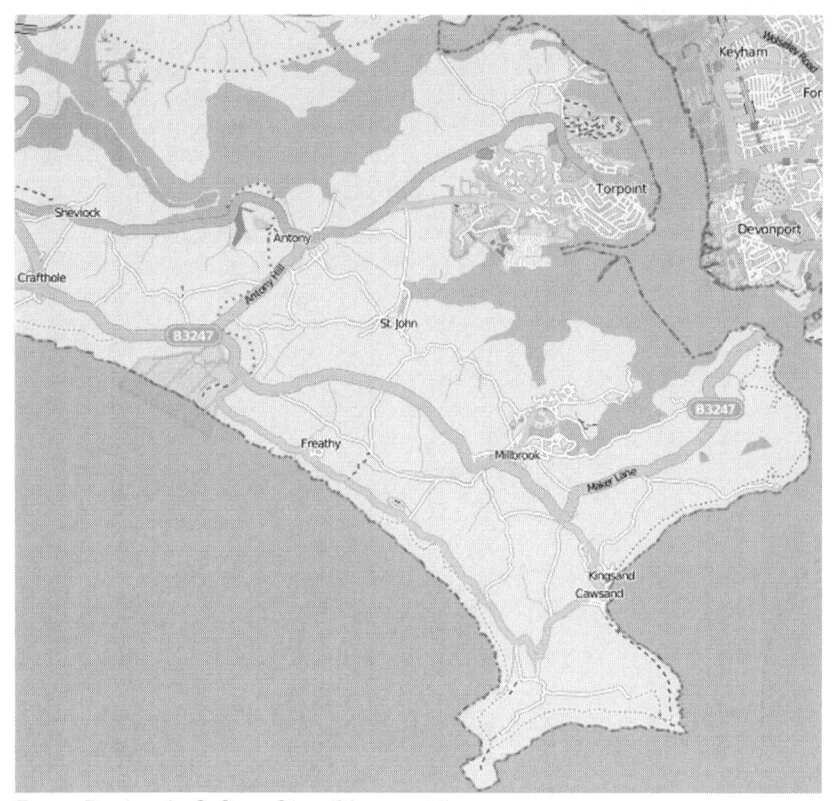

South East Cornwall: Fowey, Looe, Lostwithiel, Rame Peninsula, Polperro and Torpoint

Rame Peninsula © OpenStreetMap contributors

OUR FAVOURITES

Sheviock Barton, Torpoint (PL11 3EH) B & B

Sheviock Barton is situated in the centre of the small unspoiled village of Sheviock, directly opposite the thirteenth century church. It reputedly stands on the site of the earlier medieval manor house of Sheviock. The current 300 year-old house has been totally but sympathetically restored. All around there are large gardens and grounds, with masses of parking and an adjoining paddock.

Torpoint, PL11 3EH
01503 230793
http://www.sheviockbarton.co.uk

Buttervilla Farm, Torpoint (PL11 3EY) B & B

Buttervilla B&B exists in a bubble of peacefulness on the stunning Port Eliot Estate just a short drive from the South Cornish coast. Buttervilla offers laid back hospitality and nearby are a wealth of glorious beaches, historic houses, fine restaurants, interesting towns and quaint fishing villages, making Buttervilla the perfect place to relax and eat well.

They have fifteen idyllic acres with great views over some exceptionally beautiful rolling countryside. Buttervilla an eco-friendly, Soil Association Certified organic farm, fully equipped with modern conveniences is a very special place to stay. Rooms are spacious, en-suite, have solar heated spring water showers and very comfortable king-size or double beds. Organic teas and ground coffee, flat screen TV, free broadband wi-fi access, local maps, books and restaurant lists are all supplied in your room.

A Very Special Breakfast
Buttervilla prides itself on the quality and the local sourcing of their

food. Breakfasts feature Gill's home made bread, granola, fruit coulis, yogurt and preserves, eggs are fresh from our own chickens. Free range dry cured bacon and a Cornish speciality, hogs pudding, are supplied by a traditional local butcher. In season the tomatoes are their own super tasty heirloom varieties. Preserves are made from their own damsons, strawberries, blackcurrant's or raspberries.

Polbathic,St Germans, **Torpoint**, PL11 3EY
01503 230315
http://www.buttervilla.com

Finnygook, Torpoint (PL11 3BQ) PUB

The Finnygook is a favourite amongst those wishing to enjoy superb, freshly prepared and locally sourced food in beautiful views, whether sitting outside in the sun or next to a roaring log fire, whilst being only a stones throw from the beach. This is a top spot amongst locals and tourists alike, with the Gook Cafe also becoming a firm favourite amongst coastal path walkers and other visitors to the area.

Crafthole, **Torpoint**, PL11 3BQ
01503 230338
http://www.finnygook.co.uk/

The Old Rectory, Torpoint (PL11 3AW) B & B

Come and stay in the most sustainable B&B in Britain! The 5 star en-suite rooms are set in a Victorian Rectory powered by the sun. Feel free to roam the walled kitchen garden, enjoy a glass of wine on the secluded deck, or meet the pigs at feeding time. Open all year with evening meals on request.

St John-in-Cornwall, **Torpoint**, PL11 3AW
01752 823902

South East Cornwall: Fowey, Looe, Lostwithiel, Rame Peninsula, Polperro and Torpoint

HOTELS

A selection of superior hotels, big or small, where you can be assured of quality, comfort and a warm welcome.

The Old Quay House `HOTEL`
28 Fore Street, **Fowey**, PL23 1AQ
01726 833302
http://www.theoldquayhouse.com
Right on the water, in the centre with captivating views. Boutique hotel with elegant modern décor

The Beach House `HOTEL`
Marine Drive, Hannafore, **Looe**, PL13 2DH
01503 262598
http://www.thebeachhouselooe.co.uk

Barclay House `HOTEL`
St Martin's Road, **Looe**, PL13 1LP
01503 262929
http://www.barclayhouse.co.uk

Trelaske Hotel & Restaurant `HOTEL`
Polperro Road, **Looe**, PL13 2JS
01503 262159
http://www.trelaske.co.uk

South East Cornwall: Fowey, Looe, Lostwithiel, Rame Peninsula, Polperro and Torpoint

BED & BREAKFAST

Interesting and highly rated B&Bs with a focus on your comfort and a warm welcome.

Trevanion B & B
70 Lostwithiel Street, **Fowey**, PL23 1BQ
01726 832602
http://www.trevanionguesthouse.co.uk
Grade II listed building that dates back to the 16th Century and was at one time the Spanish Embassy.

Lesquite B & B
Lansallos, PL13 2QE
01503 220315
http://www.lesquite.co.uk
Lesquite is an attractive 17th century farmhouse in a beautiful peaceful wooded valley between Looe & Polperro.

Tredudwell Manor B & B
Lanteglos-by-Fowey, PL23 1NJ
01726 870226
http://www.tredudwellmanor.co.uk

Allhays B & B
Porthallow, Talland Bay, **Looe**, PL13 2JB
01503 273188
http://www.allhays.co.uk

Hill Farmhouse B & B
Lostwithiel, PL22 0RU
01503 220517

Bucklawren Farm B & B
St Martin, **Looe**, PL13 1NZ
01503 240738
http://www.bucklawren.com
Luxury holiday cottages.

Coombe Farm B & B
Widegates, **Looe**, PL13 1QN
01503 240223
http://www.coombefarmhotel.co.uk
Coombe Farm offers friendly hospitality in a beautiful setting, with many places of interest for all ages nearby.

Collon Barton B & B
Lerryn, **Lostwithiel**, PL22 0NX
01208 872908
Breakfast is in the farm kitchen on the biggest Cornish slate table you are ever likely to see.

Sheviock Barton B & B
Torpoint, PL11 3EH
01503 230793
http://www.sheviockbarton.co.uk
Bed & Breakfast in a beautiful, traditional farmhouse set right in the heart of Cornwall's 'forgotten corner'.

The Old Rectory B & B
St John-in-Cornwall, **Torpoint**, PL11 3AW
01752 823902

Cliff House B & B
Devonport Hill, Kingsland, **Torpoint**, PL10 1NJ
01752 823110
http://www.cliffhouse-kingsand.co.uk/
Located in the quiet unspoilt fishing village of Kingsand in Cornwall.

South East Cornwall: Fowey, Looe, Lostwithiel, Rame Peninsula, Polperro and Torpoint

Buttervilla Farm B & B
Polbathic,St Germans, **Torpoint**, PL11 3EY
01503 230315
http://www.buttervilla.com
Buttervilla is a funky farmhouse B&B situated within fifteen acres of rolling countryside.

The Bungalow B & B
Cliff Road, Portwrinkle, **Torpoint**, PL11 3BY
01503 230334
http://www.portwrinklebedandbreakfast.co.uk
"The Bungalow" B&B, Portwrinkle is nestled into the cliffs overlooking Portwrinkle village. An 18 hole golf course is adjacent to the property.

South East Cornwall: Fowey, Looe, Lostwithiel, Rame Peninsula, Polperro and Torpoint

PUBS/GASTROPUBS

Above average pubs serving quality real ale, excellent bar food or both.

The Globe Inn `PUB`
3 North Street, **Lostwithiel**, PL22 0EG
01208 872501
http://www.globeinn.com/
Excellent food, real ales and en-suite accommodation.

Rashleigh `PUB`
Polkerris, **Par**, PL24 2TL
01726 813991
http://www.therashleighinnpolkerris.co.uk/
The inn on the beach

The Blue Peter `PUB`
Quay road, **Polperro**, PL13 2QZ
01503 272743
http://www.thebluepeter.co.uk/
Good food and beer and live music.

Finnygook `PUB`
Crafthole, **Torpoint**, PL11 3BQ
01503 230338
http://www.finnygook.co.uk/

South East Cornwall: Fowey, Looe, Lostwithiel, Rame Peninsula, Polperro and Torpoint

RESTAURANTS

Only top notch restaurants are listed here. Cooking stars are drawn from "The Good Food Guide 2013".

The View ★★☆☆☆☆☆☆☆☆ RESTAURANT

Treninnow Cliff Road, **Millbrook**, PL10 1JY

www.theview-restaurant.co.uk
Great views over Whitsand Bay.

South East Cornwall: Fowey, Looe, Lostwithiel, Rame Peninsula, Polperro and Torpoint

CHURCHES

These churches all have something special and are worthy of a visit. Star ratings are from Simon Jenkin's Best Churches.

St Samson ★☆☆☆☆ CHURCH
Golant, **Fowey**, PL22 0PB

St Wyllow ★★☆☆☆ CHURCH
Lanteglos-By-Fowey, PL23 1ND

St Germanus ★★★☆☆ CHURCH
W of Saltash on railway, **St Germans**, PL12 5NJ

St Winnow ★☆☆☆☆ CHURCH
N of Golant, **St Winnow**, PL22 0LG

South East Cornwall: Fowey, Looe, Lostwithiel, Rame Peninsula, Polperro and Torpoint

HOUSES & CASTLES

Restormel Castle ★★☆☆☆ HOUSE
Restormel Road, **Lostwithiel**, PL22 0EE
01208 872687
www.english-heritage.org.uk/daysout/properties/restormel-castle/
The great 13th century circular shell-keep of Restormel still encloses the principal rooms of the castle in remarkably good condition. It stands on an earlier Norman mound surrounded by a deep dry ditch, atop a high spur beside the River Fowey. Twice visited by the Black Prince, it finally saw action during the Civil War in 1644. It commands fantastic views and is a favourite picnic spot.

Mount Edgcumbe House ★★☆☆☆ HOUSE
Cremyll, **Torpoint**, PL10 1HZ
01752 822236
http://www.plymouth.gov.uk/mountedgcumbe
Mount Edgcumbe House is a stately home. It is a Grade II listed building and the gardens are listed as Grade I in the Register of Parks and Gardens of Special Historic Interest in England.

Antony House ★★★☆☆ HOUSE
2m NW of Torpoint, **Torpoint**, PL11 2QA
01752 812191
www.nationaltrust.org.uk/antony/
Superb early 18th-century mansion set in parkland and fine gardens

South East Cornwall: Fowey, Looe, Lostwithiel, Rame Peninsula, Polperro and Torpoint

GARDENS

Gardens listed here have been rated by the "Good Gardens Guide".

Boconnoc House ★★☆☆☆ GARDEN
Lostwithiel, PL22 0RG
01208 872546
www.boconnoc.com/
The Woodland Gardens at Boconnoc are open for charity on Sundays in May and group visits for 20 people or more to the House and Garden can be arranged throughout the year. Boconnoc House is also open to visit on these days to view the extensive restoration that has taken place and to learn about the historical intrigue of the Estate and the proceeds of the Pitt Diamond that it was purchased with in 1771.

Antony House ★☆☆☆☆ GARDEN
Torpoint, PL11 2QL
01752 812364
www.nationaltrust.org.uk/antony/
The grounds bordering the Lynher estuary, landscaped by Repton, include a formal garden with topiary, a knot garden and modern sculptures. The Woodland Garden has outstanding rhododendrons, azaleas, magnolias and camellias.

Mount Edgcumbe House and Country Park
★☆☆☆☆ GARDEN
Cremyll, **Torpoint**, PL10 1HZ
01752 822236
http://www.plymouth.gov.uk/mountedgcumbe
The wider park is open year round, daily from 8am to dusk and is free to the public. The free area of the park includes the National Camellia Collection and the majority of the formal gardens.

South East Cornwall: Fowey, Looe, Lostwithiel, Rame Peninsula, Polperro and Torpoint

BEACHES

All of our beaches have the stamp of approval from the Marine Conservation Society (http://www.mcsuk.org/).

Readymoney BEACH
Fowey, PL23 1JD
Small sandy beach

Kingsand Bay Beach BEACH
Kingsand, PL10 1NF
Sand lifeguarded

Downderry Beach BEACH
Looe, PL11
Sand & shingle

Looe East BEACH
Looe, PL13 1BU
Sand rock

Portwrinkle Beach BEACH
Portwrinkle, **Looe**, PL11 3DQ
Sand rock

Cawsand Bay BEACH
Torpoint, PL10 1PD
Sand lifeguarded

South East Cornwall: Fowey, Looe, Lostwithiel, Rame Peninsula, Polperro and Torpoint

VIEWPOINTS

Polperro VIEWPOINT
Polperro, PL13 2RS

www.polperro.org/
Picturesque Cornish fishing village.

South East Cornwall: Fowey, Looe, Lostwithiel, Rame Peninsula, Polperro and Torpoint

FAMILY FUN

Monkey Sanctuary FAMILY FUN
Off B3253, E of Looe, **Looe**, PL13 1NZ
01503 262532
http://www.monkeysanctuary.org

Porfell Animal Land FAMILY FUN
Trecangate, nr Lostwithiel, **Lostwithiel**, PL14 4RE
01503 220211
http://www.chycor.co.uk/tourism/porfell

South East Cornwall: Fowey, Looe, Lostwithiel, Rame Peninsula, Polperro and Torpoint

GOLF COURSES

Courses in this guide have reached a very good standard and have something special to offer the advanced and novice player alike.

Looe Golf Club ★★☆☆☆ GOLF
Bindown, **Looe**, PL13 1PX
01503 240239
www.looegolfclub.co.uk/
Designed by six - times open champion, Harry Vardon, Looe Golf Club is set around an area of quite breathtaking beauty.

Whitsand Bay Hotel Golf Club ★☆☆☆☆ GOLF
Portwrinkle, **Torpoint**, PL11 3BU
01503 230276
www.whitsandbayhotel.co.uk/
Whitsand Bay Golf Club is one of the most stunning cliff top golf courses in Cornwall. With a distinctive landscape and rolling fairways, this 18-hole golf course was laid by Fernie of Troon in 1905 and is designed for the holiday golfer as well as the serious club golfer.

South East Cornwall: Fowey, Looe, Lostwithiel, Rame Peninsula, Polperro and Torpoint

ANTIQUES

Old Palace Antiques ANTIQUES
Quay Street, **Lostwithiel**, PL22 0BS
01208 782909

Uzella Court Antiques & Fine Art ANTIQUES
2 Fore Street, **Lostwithiel**, PL22 0BP
01208 872255
http://www.uzellacourtantiques.com/

South West Cornwall: Falmouth, Mevagissey, Penryn, St Austell and Truro

Falmouth is situated at the mouth of the Fal on a harbour that is the third deepest in the world and the deepest in Europe. The Falmouth Packet Service operated out of Falmouth for over 160 years between 1689 and 1851 to carry the mails to the expanding Empire and as the south western most harbour it was often a first port of call for returning Royal Navy ships. The National Maritime Museum, opened in 2003, is very good indeed. Tourism is now the main industry but the docks and Her Majesty's Coast Guard as well as a great many yachts mean that the sea is still central to its economy. Pendennis Castle and its opposite number in St Mawes were built by Henry VIII to protect Carrick Roads from French and Spanish attack. A foot ferry now joins the two headlands.

Trebah , 4½ miles SW of Falmouth is 25 magic acres as only Cornwall can do. On the banks of the Helford River it has a collection of sub-tropical Mediterranean plants. Its history of grandeur, decline and rebirth is fascinating.

St Mawes has a fine harbour with a castle (see above) and is popular with the sailing fraternity. Second homes and tourism are the main supports of the economy. Tresanton is a well liked upscale hotel owned by Olga Polizzi (née Forte).

Mevagissey is an old fishing port of small streets and tourists who have largely supplanted fishing. There is a ferry to Falmouth which is a nice way to spend time, and there is the World of Model Railways for boys of all ages. Nearby are two of the finest gardens in the land – the Lost Gardens of Heligan started in the 18th C but neglected since 1914 and resurrected by Tim Smit of Eden Project fame. This 200 acre garden has too much to describe – just go, you will not regret it. The other garden is Caerhays Castle – unsurpassed in spring and one of the greatest of all British gardens.

Penryn is a much older town than adjacent Falmouth which usurped its earlier pre-eminence. It has retained a large part of its heritage and has been designated an important conservation area.

St Austell with a population of over 30,000 is the largest town in Cornwall. Its size is the product of China clay discovered by William Cookworthy in 1746 at Tregonning Hill. The country about St Austell has the largest reserves of top grade China clay outside China. The industry grew as tin mining declined and many came to St Austell to find work. Many fewer are employed now in China clay mining but the volume is larger than ever

Ten miles south is *Caerhays Castle* in a setting as romantic as its architectural style by John Nash. The garden is one of the finest in Britain, and the home of the national magnolia collection.

Just beyond it is *Dodman Point*, a strong contender as the most rugged of capes in a county not short of them.

Eden Project is the initiative of the redoubtable Tim Smit. The two great geodesic biomes (super greenhouses) contain in one a tropical rain forest and in the other a Mediterranean environment. The temperate zone is not covered. It is educational and recreational – unique in the world; must visit at least once.

Roseland is a fine example of the soft side of Cornwall. The rock-hard sun-and –showers of the county's spine seems far away.

Probus lies on the River Fal, off the A390 on the St Austell side of Truro is famous for having the highest tower in Cornwall, 125 feet, and perhaps the finest. The locals, thwarted by their landlord sought help from Somerset – so here is a bit of South Petherton in granite rather than limestone. In the church vestry is a real treasure, a monument to Thomas Hawkins (d.1766) owner of the local mansion of Trewithen. It is Georgian and grand enough for Westminster Abbey.

Truro is the county town pop. 20.000 therefore second in size to St Austell. Originally it was a more important port than Falmouth but as the river silted up it had a poor 17th C but tin mining rescued it in the 18th C and hence the pleasant Georgian houses. The cathedral 1880-

1910 is Early English/ French in style built of Cornish granite and Bath stone. This style owes little to its surroundings but is still impressive. It was built where the church of St Mary's previously existed, a challenging site to (almost) conform to which leaves it without the usual cathedral close. In summer there are five wonderfully scenic boat trips a day along the rivers to Falmouth.

Veryan has housing built by the Rector about 200 years ago. He built them round so that the Devil would have no corners to hide in. His theology may not have worn well but his architecture has enduring charm.

South West Cornwall: Falmouth, Mevagissey, Penryn, St Austell and Truro

Lighthouse in Falmouth

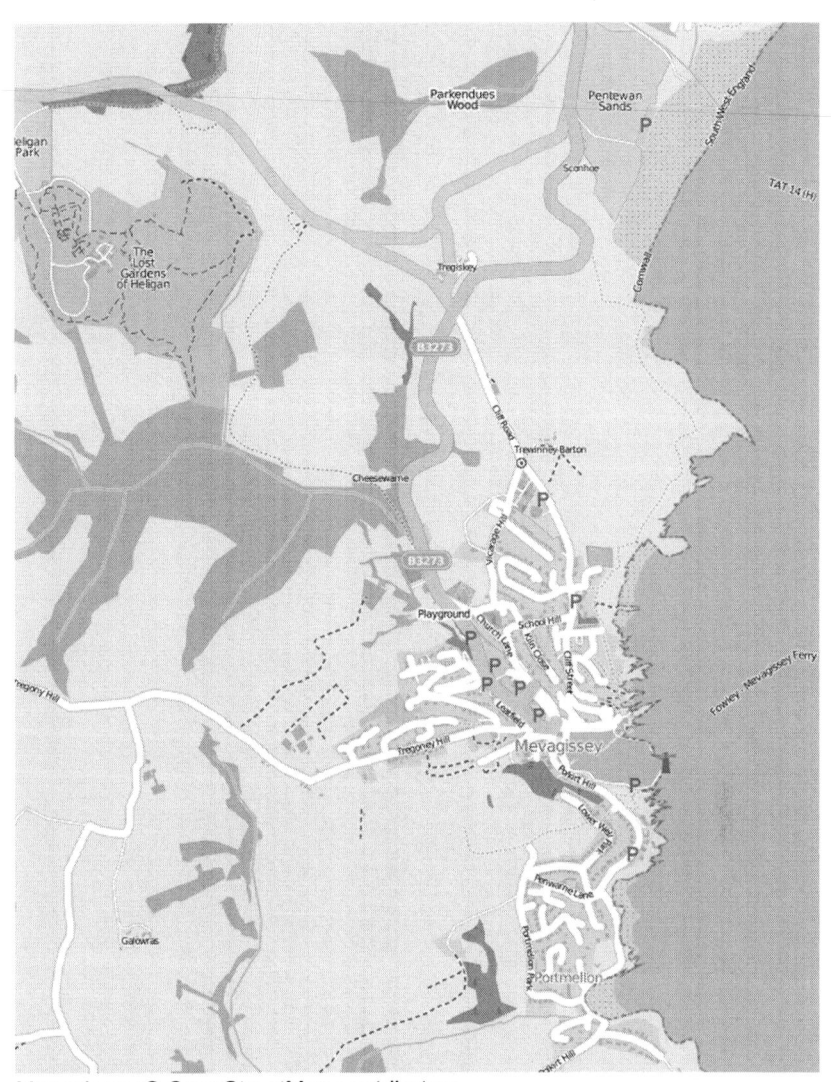

Mevagissey © OpenStreetMap contributors

South West Cornwall: Falmouth, Mevagissey, Penryn, St Austell and Truro

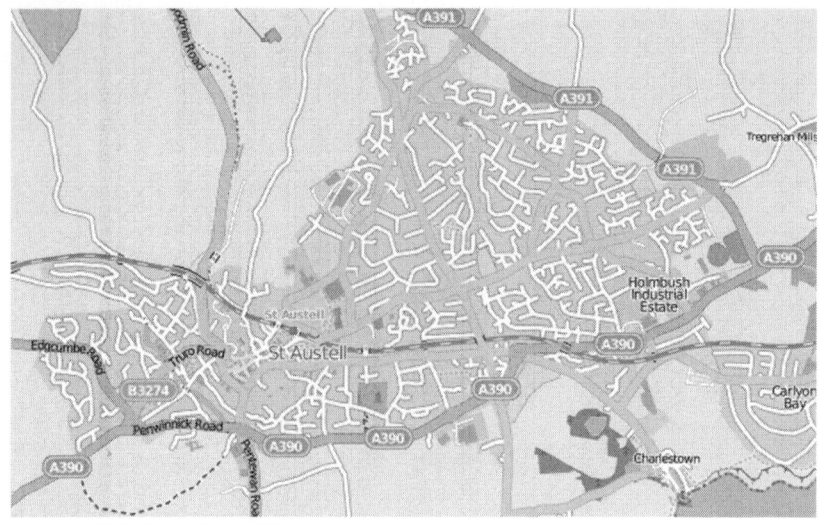

St Austell © OpenStreetMap contributors

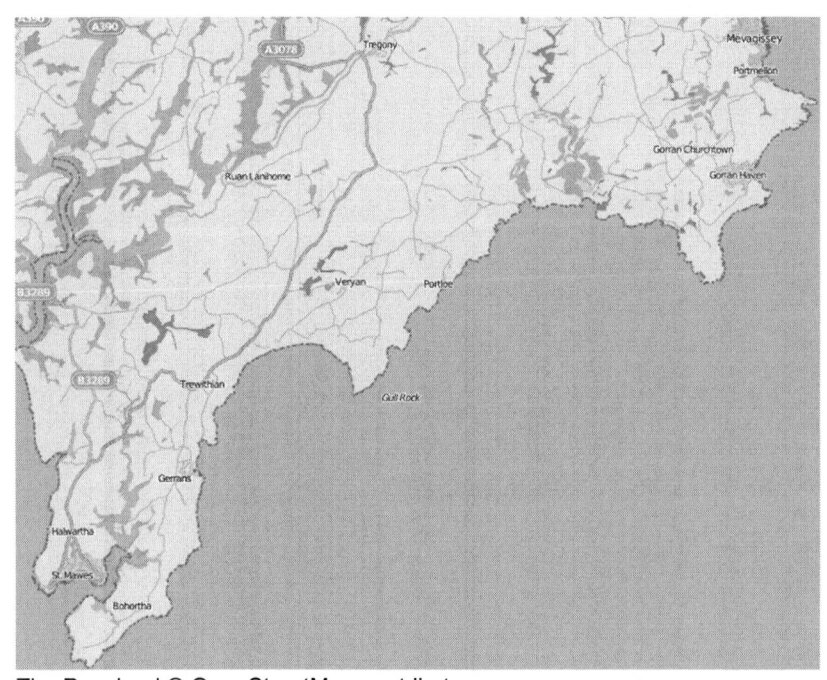

The Roseland © OpenStreetMap contributors

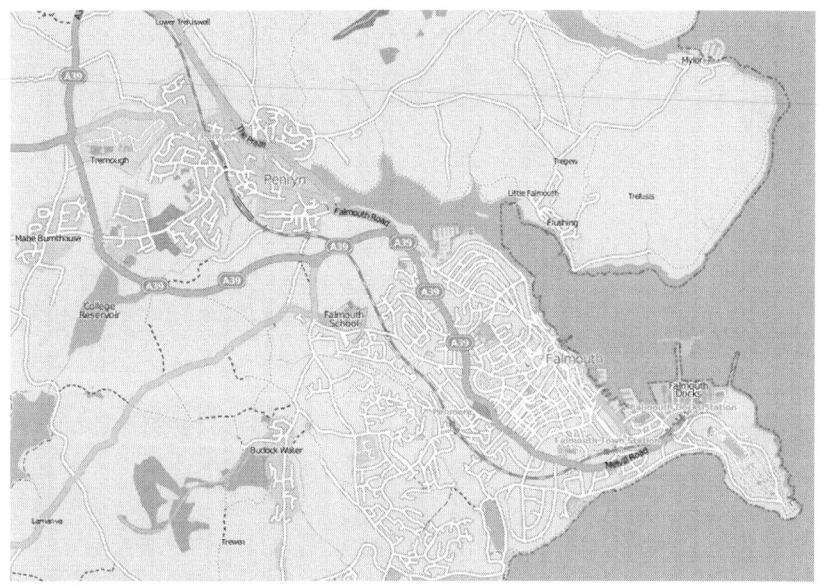

South West Cornwall: Falmouth, Mevagissey, Penryn, St Austell and Truro

Falmouth © OpenStreetMap contributors

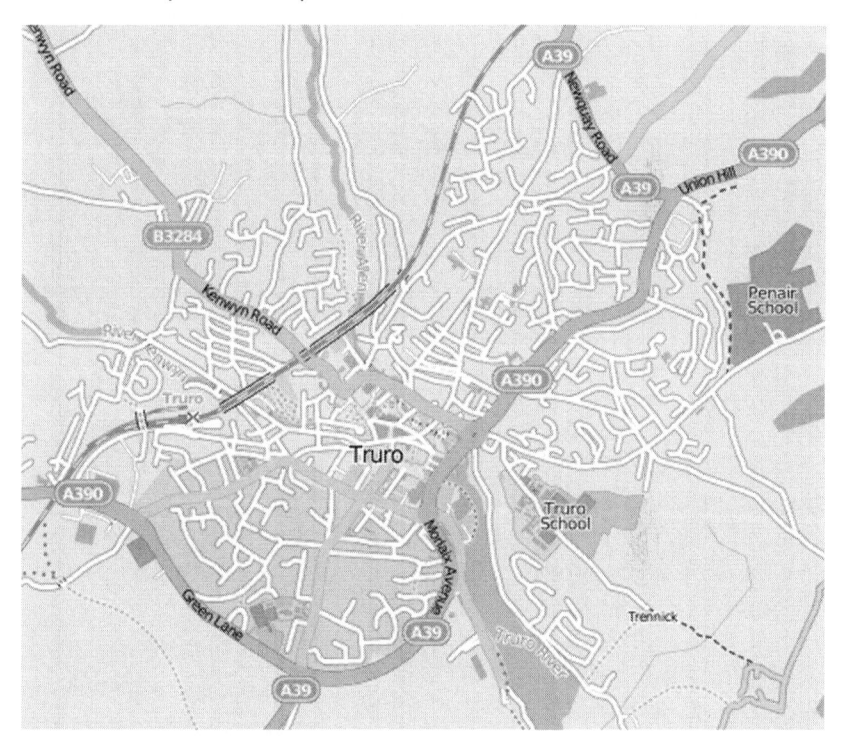

Truro © OpenStreetMap contributors

OUR FAVOURITES

Nanscawen Manor House, St Blazey (PL24 2SR)
B & B

Nanscawen Manor House is a delightful country house set in an idyllic location. Only 2 Miles from The Eden Project. It stands in 5 acres of grounds & gardens with lovely views Southward over a valley. There are Four luxury en-suite rooms all bathrooms have spa baths and 3 with showers. The elegantly furnished drawing room leads into the conservatory where breakfast is enjoyed. You are welcome to enjoy the peaceful, tranquil beauty of the gardens. The large outdoor swimming pool is heated and has wonderful views to the South over unspoilt country side. This is available from Mid May through to Mid September.

Guests may luxuriate in the hot spa tub, which is beside the pool and is heated to 97f, this is available in the summer months. We look forward welcoming you to our home. Many good restaurants are within easy reach. An ideal base for touring all of Cornwall. Places to visit- Heligan garden 8 miles, Fowey 5 miles, Lanhydrock House 6 miles.

Luxulyan Valley, **St Blazey**, PL24 2SR
01726 814488
http://www.nanscawen.com

Old Quay, Truro (TR3 6NE) PUB

This long established traditional pub, at the head of Restronguet Creek, adjacent to the coast-to-coast trail, is enjoying a renaissance under owners Hannah and John Calland. Chef Alex, who trained at The Ivy, creates seriously good food, weaving together the best of local produce into an imaginative daily specials menu with a modern twist. There are well-chosen wines and local beers, to enjoy and the garden could be called Devoran's best-kept secret. Families and man's best freinds welcome. Open from 11am daily.

Devoran, **Truro**, TR3 6NE
01872 863142
http://www.theoldquayinn.co.uk/

Hay Barton, Treworga (TR2 5TF) B & B

Hay Barton Bed and Breakfast is situated at the top of the Roseland Peninsular, surrounded by its own fields making it peaceful yet only 15 minites to The Lost Gardens of Heligan, St Mawes and Truro. They serve delicious locally sourced breakfasts. Guests are welcomed with cake to enjoy in their own sitting room or outside in summer.

Tregony, **Treworga**, TR2 5TF
01872 530288
http://www.haybarton.com

South West Cornwall: Falmouth, Mevagissey, Penryn, St Austell and Truro

HOTELS

A selection of superior hotels, big or small, where you can be assured of quality, comfort and a warm welcome.

The Greenbank HOTEL
Harbourside, **Falmouth**, TR11 2SR
01326 312440
http://www.greenbank-hotel.co.uk

The Rosemary HOTEL
22 Gyllyngvase Terrace, **Falmouth**, TR11 4DL
01326 314669
http://www.therosemary.co.uk

Budock Vean HOTEL
Helford Passage, **Mawnan Smith**, TR11 5LG
01326 252100
http://www.budockvean.co.uk

Meudon HOTEL
Mawnan Smith, TR11 5HT
01326 250541
http://www.meudon.co.uk

The Llawnroc HOTEL
Chute Lane, Gorran Haven, **Mevagissey**, PL26 6NU
01726 843461
http://www.thellawnrochotel.co.uk/

Trevalsa Court HOTEL
School Hill, **Mevagissey**, PL26 6TH
01726 842468
http://www.trevalsa-hotel.co.uk

Driftwood Hotel HOTEL
Rosevine, **Portscatho**, TR2 5EW
01872 580644
http://www.driftwoodhotel.co.uk

Hotel Tresanton HOTEL
27 Lower Castle Road, **St Mawes**, TR2 5DR
01326 270055
http://www.tresanton.com

The Nare HOTEL
Carne Beach, **Veryan-in-Roseland**, TR2 5PF
01872 501111
http://www.narehotel.co.uk

South West Cornwall: Falmouth, Mevagissey, Penryn, St Austell and Truro

BED & BREAKFAST

Interesting and highly rated B&Bs with a focus on your comfort and a warm welcome.

Tregew Vean B & B
Flushing, **Falmouth**, TR11 5TF
01326 379462
http://www.tregewvean.co.uk/
TREGEW VEAN is an attractive 1760's Packet Skipper's house in the idyllic waterside village of Flushing, facing Falmouth.

Bosvathick B & B
Constantine, **Falmouth**, TR11 5RD
01326 340103
http://www.bosvathickhouse.co.uk/
This Grade II listed Georgian house is close to the south Cornish coast in an area of outstanding natural beauty, within very easy reach of numerous creeks, estuaries and beaches.

Bissick Old Mill B & B
Ladock, TR2 4PG
01726 882557
http://www.bissickoldmill.co.uk
A small luxury guesthouse.

Portmellon Cove B & B
121 Portmellon Park, **Mevagissey**, PL26 6XD
01726 843410
http://www.portmellon-cove.com
Award winning accommodation with beautiful sea views.

Bodrugan Barton B & B
Mevagissey, PL26 6PT
01726 842094
http://www.bodrugan.co.uk
Sparkling sea and a rolling landscape provide the backdrop for a self-catering cottage holiday.

Ancient Shipbrokers B & B
Higher West End, **Pentewan**, PL26 6BY
01726 843370
http://www.pentewanbedandbreakfast.com/
Ancient Shipbrokers offers comfort, privacy and tranquillity in the centre of Pentewan village.

Trenderway Farm B & B
Pelynt, **Portloe**, PL13 2LY
01503 272214
http://trenderwayfarmholidays.co.uk
A romantic 5 Star Cornish haven, Trenderway Farm offers couples a perfect Cornish holiday on a beautiful working farm.

Hunters Moon B & B
Chapel Hill, Polgooth,, **St Austell**, PL26 7BU
01726 66445
http://www.huntersmooncornwall.co.uk

Anchorage House B & B
Boscundle, **St Austell**, PL25 3RH
01726 814071
http://www.anchoragehouse.co.uk
Luxurious and small adults only B&B.

Gardens Cottage B & B
Prideaux, Parl, **St Austell**, PL24 2SS
01726 817195
http://www.gardenscottage.co.uk
Gardens Cottage offers rural charm with modern luxury.

Tubbs Mill House B & B
Caerhays, Gorran, **St Austell**, PL26 6NB
01872 530715
http://www.cornwall-online.co.uk/tubbs-mill/
Bed & Breakfast in a 300 year Old Mill House. Peaceful and secluded valley setting.

Poltarrow Farm B & B
St Mewan, **St Austell**, PL26 7DR
01726 67111
http://www.poltarrow.co.uk
Farmhouse Bed and Breakfast and Self Catering holiday cottages.

Nanscawen Manor House B & B
Luxulyan Valley, **St Blazey**, PL24 2SR
01726 814488
http://www.nanscawen.com
Luxury B&B near the Eden Project.

Penarwyn House B & B
Par, **St Blazey**, PL24 2DS
01726 814224
http://www.penarwyn.co.uk
Large Victorian gentleman's residence offering B&B in style.

Braganza B & B
St Mawes, TR2 5BJ
01326 270281
http://braganza-stmawes.co.uk/
Braganza B&B is an elegant Regency House built around 1800.

Pelyn B & B
Gerrans, Portscatho, **Treworga**, TR2 5ET
01872 580837
http://www.pelyncreek.com
Pelyn B&B offers peace and relaxation - a place to unwind.

Little Roseland B & B
Ruan Highlanes, **Treworga**, TR2 5NP
01872 501243
http://www.littleroseland.co.uk
Little Roseland is a traditional Cornish house dating from 1704 in the heart of the hamlet Treworga in the middle of Cornwall's stunning Roseland Peninsula. Offers excellent service B&B.

Hay Barton B & B
Tregony, **Treworga**, TR2 5TF
01872 530288
http://www.haybarton.com
Hay Barton farmhouse B&B is quiet and tranquil and the perfect place to relax and unwind.

Tregoose B & B
Grampound, **Treworga**, TR2 4BD
01726 882460
http://www.tregoose.co.uk
Tregoose is a Regency Cornish country house offering traditional B&B with dinner by arrangement.

Trevilla House B & B
Feock, **Treworga**, TR3 6QG
01872 862369
http://www.trevilla.com
Home cooking, spacious rooms and wonderful views make this B&B a very relaxing place to stay.

Oxturn House B & B
Ladock, **Treworga**, TR2 4NQ
01726 884348
http://www.oxturnhouse.co.uk
Good quality traditional B&B.

Bosillion B & B
Bosillion Lane, Grampound, **Truro**, TR2 4QY
01726 883327

Manor Cottage B & B
Tresillian, **Truro**, TR2 4BN
01872 520212
http://www.manorcottage.com
The guest house and its rooms are comfortable, warm and friendly and the family go out of their way to make you feel at home.

South West Cornwall: Falmouth, Mevagissey, Penryn, St Austell and Truro

PUBS/GASTROPUBS

Above average pubs serving quality real ale, excellent bar food or both.

Trengilly Wartha Inn PUB
Nancenoy, Contstantine, **Falmouth**, TR11 5RP
01326 340332
www.trengilly.co.uk/
Country Inn and restaurant. Best family pub of the year 2011 in the West Country (Morning Advertiser).

Pandora PUB
Restronguet Creek, **Mylor Bridge**, TR11 5ST
01326 372678
http://www.pandorainn.com/
Spectacular setting on the edge of Restronguet Creek. Real ales and fresh local food.

Royal Oak Freehouse and Restaurant PUB
Perranwell, TR3 7PX
01872 863175
http://www.royaloakperranwell.co.uk
A charming and welcoming country pub in the village of Perranwell Station.

Roseland Inn PUB
Philleigh-in-Roseland, **Truro**, TR2 5NB
01872 580254
http://www.roselandinn.co.uk/
A truly traditional Cornish pub.

Old Quay PUB
Devoran, **Truro**, TR3 6NE
01872 863142
http://www.theoldquayinn.co.uk/
Lovely pub uphill from the quay but just yards from the Portreath-Devoran mineral tramway

South West Cornwall: Falmouth, Mevagissey, Penryn, St Austell and Truro

RESTAURANTS

Only top notch restaurants are listed here. Cooking stars are drawn from "The Good Food Guide 2013".

Helford Passage ★★☆☆☆☆☆☆☆☆ RESTAURANT
Helford Passage, TR11 5LB
01326 250625
http://www.ferryboatinnhelford.com
Wright Brothers seafood specialities alongside home-made classics.

Driftwood ★★★★★☆☆☆☆☆ RESTAURANT
Rosevine, **Portscatho**, TR2 5EW
01872 580644
http://www.driftwoodhotel.co.uk
Clifftop hotel, stylish food. With a Michelin star.

Rosevine ★★☆☆☆☆☆☆☆☆ RESTAURANT
Portscatho, TR2 5EW
www.rosevine.co.uk
A great little restaurant with sea views, overlooking Gerrans Bay. Modern country style food, locally grown and seasonal.

Hotel Tresanton ★★★☆☆☆☆☆☆☆ RESTAURANT
Lower Castle Road, **St Mawes**, TR2 5DR
01326 270055
http://www.tresanton.com
Stylish seaside escape.

Tabb's ★★★★☆☆☆☆☆☆ RESTAURANT
85 Kenwyn Street, **Truro**, TR1 3BZ
01872 262110

http://www.tabbs.co.uk
Homely feel with daring food.

CHURCHES

These churches all have something special and are worthy of a visit. Star ratings are from Simon Jenkin's Best Churches.

St Mylor ★☆☆☆☆ CHURCH
Mylor Churchtown, **Falmouth**, TR11 5UG

Holy Trinity ★☆☆☆☆ CHURCH
St Austell, PL25 4NT

St Just-in-Roseland ★☆☆☆☆ CHURCH
N of St Mawes, **St Just-in-Roseland**, TR2 5JE

St Anthony ★☆☆☆☆ CHURCH
St Anthony-in-Roseland, **St Mawes**, TR2 5EY

St Probus and St Grace ★★☆☆☆ CHURCH
Probus, **Truro**, TR2 4ND

Famous for having the tallest church tower in Cornwall. It stands at 129 ft (39m) high.

Quaker Meeting House ★☆☆☆☆ CHURCH
Come-To-Good, **Truro**, TR3 6JD

Truro Cathedral CHURCH
Truro, TR1 2EA

South West Cornwall: Falmouth, Mevagissey, Penryn, St Austell and Truro

HOUSES & CASTLES

Pendennis Castle ★☆☆☆☆ HOUSE
Castle Close, **Falmouth**, TR11 4LP
01326 316594
www.english-heritage.org.uk/daysout/properties/pendennis-castle/
Pendennis Castle is one of Henry VIII's Device Forts, or Henrician castle, in the English county of Cornwall. It was built in 1539 for King Henry VIII to guard the entrance to the River Fal on its west bank, near Falmouth.

Caerhays Castle ★★☆☆☆ HOUSE
Gorran Churchtown, **St Austell**, PL26 6LY
01872 501310
www.caerhays.co.uk/
You can visit the castle and gardens, walk in the grounds and visit the stunning beaches which make up the estate.

St Mawes Castle ★☆☆☆☆ HOUSE
Castle Drive, **Truro**, TR2 5DE
01326 270526
www.english-heritage.org.uk/daysout/properties/st-mawes-castle/
St Mawes Castle is among the best-preserved of Henry VIII's coastal artillery fortresses, and the most elaborately decorated of them all. One of the chain of forts built between 1539 and 1545 to counter an invasion threat from Catholic France and Spain, it guarded the important anchorage of Carrick Roads, sharing the task with Pendennis Castle on the other side of the Fal estuary.

South West Cornwall: Falmouth, Mevagissey, Penryn, St Austell and Truro

GARDENS

Gardens listed here have been rated by the "Good Gardens Guide".

Trebah ★★☆☆☆ GARDEN
Mawnan Smith, **Falmouth**, TR11 5JZ
01326 252500
www.trebahgarden.co.uk/
A sub-tropical paradise with a stunning coastal backdrop. Open every day of the year, from 10am.

Carwinion Garden GARDEN
Mawnan Smith, **Falmouth**, TR11 5JA
01326 250258
http://www.carwinion.co.uk
Nature lovers from around the world visit Carwinion to admire its renowned collection of bamboo and to relax among the beautiful and rare plants in these 14 acres of tranquil garden.

Glendurgan Garden ★☆☆☆☆ GARDEN
Mawnan Smith, **Falmouth**, TR11 5JZ
01326 250906
www.nationaltrust.org.uk/glendurgan-garden/
Superb subtropical garden, with special interest for families

Lost Gardens of Heligan ★★☆☆☆ GARDEN
Pentewan, **St Austell**, PL26 6EN
01726 845100
www.heligan.com/
Heligan offers over 200 acres for exploration. Discover the Victorian Productive Gardens, romantic Pleasure Grounds, lush sub-tropical Jungle, pioneering Wildlife Project & beyond...

Caerhays Castle Garden ★★☆☆☆ GARDEN
Gorran, **St Austell**, PL26 6LY
01872 501310
http://www.caerhays.co.uk/
Caerhays has an international reputation for its camellias and rhododendrons and is home to a national magnolia collection.

Pinetum Park and Pine Lodge Gardens ★☆☆☆☆ GARDEN
Holmbush, **St Austell**, PL25 3RQ
01726 73500
http://www.pinetumpark.com/
With over 6000 labelled plants, Pinetum Park is a testament to the dedication and enthusiasm of amateur horticulturists Ray and Shirley Clemo a who travelled the world collecting seeds and plants to establish this remarkable Garden.

Marsh Villa Gardens ★☆☆☆☆ GARDEN
St Andrews Road, **St Austell**, PL24 2LU
01726 815920
www.marshvillagardens.co.uk/
This magical 3-acre water and woodland garden lies in a former tidal creek, and is rich in variety and conservational significance. With the first plantings in 1988, the garden is well established, boasting extensive herbaceous borders and mixed beds, amongst a charming network of waterways which drain the Treesmill marsh levels.

Tregrehan ★☆☆☆☆ GARDEN
Par, **St Austell**, PL24 2SJ
01726 814389
tregrehan.org/
Tregrehan Garden, although historical its approach is fresh with an extraordinary recent collection worthy of its relationship with Kew. The gardens intense privacy baffles some visitors, but reflects a character that each generation of Carlyon gardener has unfailingly brought with

him or her. Tregrehan Garden is about plants.

Lamorran House Gardens ★☆☆☆☆ GARDEN
Upper Castle Road, **St Mawes**, TR2 5BZ
01326 270800
www.lamorrangarden.co.uk/

Bosvigo Gardens ★☆☆☆☆ GARDEN
Bosvigo Lane, **Truro**, TR1 3NH
01872 275774
http://www.bosvigo.com/
Created by the Artist owner with dazzling displays of vivid colour and plant harmonies from February to October. Spring bulbs and Hellebores, summer herbaceous borders, autumn finale of 'firework' colours. House open for pre-arranged parties.

Chyverton Nature Reserve ★☆☆☆☆ GARDEN
Zelah, **Truro**, TR4 9HD
01872 540234
http://www.cornwallwildlifetrust.org.uk/
The reserve consists of flower-rich meadows, ancient Cornish hedgerows, areas of mixed woodland and a scrape; a shallow pool. In the past the site had become overgrown and the heathland was reverting to woodland, but through a combination of scrub clearance and grazing, the heathland is now being maintained. Because the meadows have been largely unimproved for agricultural purposes, they provide a variety of habitats for a diverse range of wildlife.

Creed House Gardens GARDEN
Grampound, **Truro**, TR2 4SL
01872 530372
http://www.gardensofcornwall.com/outdoor-kids/creed-house-gardens-p466313
Set foot in this five-acres of landscaped gardens and seek out many hidden corners amongst the colourful blooms.

Trelissick Garden ★☆☆☆☆ GARDEN
Feock, **Truro**, TR3 6QL
01872 862090
www.nationaltrust.org.uk/trelissick-garden/
Tranquil varied garden in fabulous position, with a superb collection of tender and exotic plants

Trewithen ★★☆☆☆ GARDEN
Grampound, **Truro**, TR2 4DD
01726 883647
http://www.trewithengardens.co.uk
Trewithen is an historic private estate internationally renowned for its collection of magnolias and camellias. Boasting 24 'Champion Trees', woodland walks, 18th Century estate house which is open to visitors on occasion throughout the year, Tea Shop and highly prized plants from the on-site nursery.

BEACHES

All of our beaches have the stamp of approval from the Marine Conservation Society (http://www.mcsuk.org/).

Maen Porth BEACH
Falmouth, TR11 5HN
Sand

Gyllyngvase BEACH
Falmouth, TR11 4NY
Spacious sands lifeguarded

Swanpool BEACH
Falmouth, TR11 5BG
Sandy cove, pebbles

Gorran Haven Vault Beach BEACH
Mevagissey, PL26
Vault Beach is a sheltered beach to the eastern side of Dodman Point which reaches up 110 metres. It is a curved sweep of sand and shingle that gently slopes into the sea. The sea here is usually pretty calm and bathing is generally safe, although there is no lifeguard patrol.

Polstreath BEACH
Mevagissey, PL26 6TE
Sand

Pentewan Sands BEACH
Mevagissey, PL26 6BT
Sand currents

Duporth Beach BEACH
St Austell, PL26 6AQ
Privately owned, sandy, access on foot from Charlestown

Crinnis Beach Golf Links BEACH
Carlyon Bay, **St Austell**, PL25 3RG
Over a mile of sand

Porthpean BEACH
St Austell, PL26 6AU
Sand

Charlestown BEACH
St Austell, PL25 3NX
Pebbles

Pendower Beach BEACH
Veryan, TR2 5EW
Mile of sand

VIEWPOINTS

Pendennis Point VIEWPOINT
Falmouth, TR11 4NQ

Pendennis Point has the most spectacular views across Falmouth Bay, from St. Anthony Lighthouse to the east and the Lizard to the west.

Zone Point VIEWPOINT
St Mawes, TR2 5HA

Zone Point is the southernmost extremity of the Roseland peninsula. The cliffs make the beach between Zone Point and St Anthony Head inaccessible from land and the small bay is the site of many Atlantic Grey Seal sightings.

South West Cornwall: Falmouth, Mevagissey, Penryn, St Austell and Truro

MUSEUMS

National Maritime Museum ★★★☆☆ MUSEUM
Discovery Quay, **Falmouth**, TR11 3SA
01326 313388
http://www.nmmc.co.uk

Royal Cornwall Museum ★★☆☆☆ MUSEUM
River Street, **Truro**, TR21 2SJ
01872 272205
http://www.royalcornwallmuseum.org.co.uk

FAMILY FUN

World of Model Railways FAMILY FUN
Mevagissey, **Mevagissey**, PL26 6UL
01726 842457

China Clay Country Park FAMILY FUN
St Austell B3274, **St Austell**, PL26 8XG
01726 850362
http://www.wheal-martyn.com

Charlestown Shipwreck Centre FAMILY FUN
Charlestown Road, **St Austell**, PL25 3NJ
01726 69897
http://www.shipwreckcharlestown.com
The many and varied exhibitions reflect village life in Charlestown, it's history, shipwrecks and the once thriving China Clay industry. The exhibition shows a tremendous range of maritime history dating back to 1715 and one of the largest underwater diving equipment collections in the country, including various suits used for treasure seeking and naval purposes.

Eden Project FAMILY FUN
Bodelva, **St Austell**, PL24 2SG
01726 811911
http://www.edenproject.com
The world's largest rainforest in captivity with steamy jungles and waterfalls * cutting-edge architecture and buildings * stunning garden displays all year round * world-class sculpture and art * evening gigs, concerts and an ice rink in the winter * educational centre and demonstrations to inspire all ages * brilliant local, fairly traded food in the restaurants and cafes * a rainforest lookout that takes you above the treetops * free land train pulled by a tractor.

GOLF COURSES

Courses in this guide have reached a very good standard and have something special to offer the advanced and novice player alike.

Falmouth Golf Club ★★☆☆☆ GOLF
Swanpool Road, **Falmouth**, TR11 5BQ
01326 311262
www.falmouthgolfclub.com/
Falmouth Golf Club welcomes all visitors and societies to their established par 71 golf course which winds its way along Cornish cliff tops with stunning views across Falmouth Bay, in the southern part of Cornwall.

St Austell Golf Club ★★☆☆☆ GOLF
Tregongeeves, **St Austell**, PL26 7DS
01726 74756
www.staustellgolf.co.uk/
An 18 hole, 6,042 yard par 69 parkland course with wonderful countryside views - a challenge to golfers of all levels!

Carlyon Bay Golf Club ★★★★☆ GOLF
Sea Road, Carlyon Bay, **St Austell**, PL25 3RD
01726 814250
www.carlyongolf.com/
The Championship golf course on the cliffs at Carlyon Bay is at once beautiful, dramatic and challenging. Stretching along the coastline towards the port of Par, the course offers 6,500 yards of the most stimulating golf in Cornwall, a comfortable club house and an extensive pro shop.

South West Cornwall: Falmouth, Mevagissey, Penryn, St Austell and Truro

NATURAL PRODUCE

Duchy of Cornwall Oyster Farm
NATURAL PRODUCE

Port Navas, **Falmouth**, TR11 5RJ
01326 340210
http://www.duchyoysterfarm.com
Oysters, mussels

Boddington's **NATURAL PRODUCE**

The Ashes, Tregony Hill, **Mevagissey**, PL26 6RQ
01726 842346
http://www.boddingtonsberries.co.uk
Specialist strawberry growers + jams

Cornish Cuisine **NATURAL PRODUCE**

Ilsington Wharf, Penryn, **Penryn**, TR10 8AT
01326 376244
http://www.cornishcuisine.co.uk
Award winning smoked fish & meat

The Crib Box **NATURAL PRODUCE**

5 Mount Charles Road, St Austell, **St Austell**, PL35 3LB
01726 64120
Pasties, sausage rolls, pies

The Cheese Shop **NATURAL PRODUCE**

29 Ferris Town, Truro, **Truro**, TR1 3JH
01872 270742
http://www.cheese-eshop.com
Only specialist cheese shop in Cornwall

Cusgarne Organic Farm NATURAL PRODUCE
Cusgarne Wollas, **Truro**, TR4 8RL
01872 865922
http://www.cusgarneorganicfarm.co.uk/
Award wining fruit & veg, chickens

Baker Tom NATURAL PRODUCE
Lemon Street, **Truro**, TR15 3SF
01209 218989
http://www.bakertom.co.uk
Award wining bakery and café.

Lizard Peninsula

Helston pop.10,600 was a stannary town as witnessed by the name 'Coinagehall Street' where the famous Floral(Furry) Dance starts. This 8 May ritual is the highlight of the Helston year. It is a marathon effort but rather more formal than the Padstow 'obby oss'. The bands are normal brass marching bands rather than the accordions of Padstow and the men wear white shirts and the women smart frocks. The dance is processional with lots of added twirls and a tendency to spin off down alleys and into and through houses. The 600 year old Blue Anchor Pub at the foot of the street plays a big part – open all night and day selling its own brew 'Spingo' beer – a favourite with real ale fans. Only in Cornwall do such things happen in Britain.

Porthleven has a good harbour packed with fishing boats and a restaurant described in the Good Food Guide as a 'little gem'. There are a few more boats in Mullion but otherwise makes a good base for beaches and coves.

Cadgwith Cove nearby is tiny working fishing port where you can see everything while standing outside the good pub.

The Lizard if you were expecting much is an anticlimax. The only attraction is the mile long track to Lizard Point and a plain lighthouse. It is a contrast to the dross surrounding Land's End.

Polbream Cove, Lizard Point

Lizard Peninsula

Lizard Peninsula © OpenStreetMap contributors

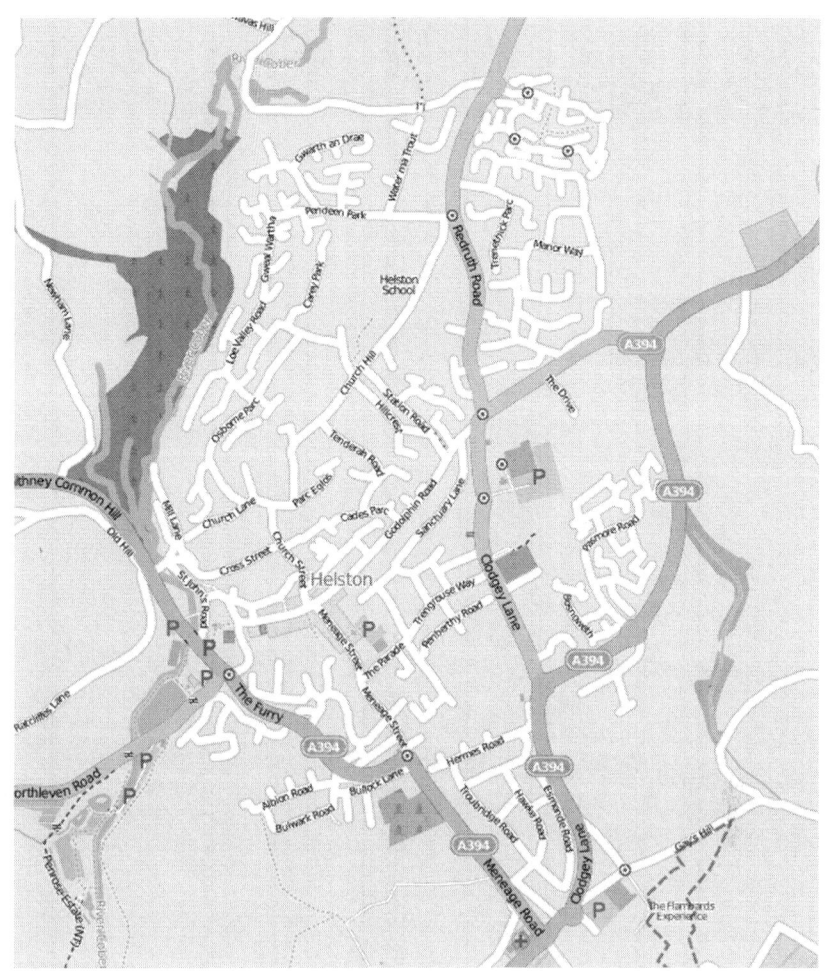

Lizard Peninsula

Helston © OpenStreetMap contributors

OUR FAVOURITES

Mullion Cove Hotel, Helston (TR12 7EP) HOTEL

The recently refurbished Mullion Cove Hotel is set in a magnificent cliff top location with stunning sea views this is truly a haven of peace and relaxation. It combines a relaxed atmosphere with friendly service and outstanding food using the very best fresh local produce. The welcome is warm and sincere, the service professional yet relaxed combining traditional values and modern amenities. The Lizard peninsula is a haven for walkers and bird watchers alike, Mullion Golf course is just two miles away and a host of fabulous Cornish Gardens are nearby.

Mullion, **Helston**, TR12 7EP
01326 240328
http://www.mullion-cove.co.uk

HOTELS

A selection of superior hotels, big or small, where you can be assured of quality, comfort and a warm welcome.

The Bay Hotel `HOTEL`
North Corner, **Coverack**, TR12 6TF
01326 280464
http://www.thebayhotel.co.uk

Mullion Cove Hotel `HOTEL`
Mullion, **Helston**, TR12 7EP
01326 240328
http://www.mullion-cove.co.uk

BED & BREAKFAST

Interesting and highly rated B&Bs with a focus on your comfort and a warm welcome.

Carmelin B & B
Pentreath Lane, The Lizard, **Helston**, TR12 7NY
01326 290677
http://www.bedandbreakfastcornwall.co.uk
The Carmelin Suite is the only accommodation available, so you do not share your holiday with any other guests.

The Gardens B & B
Tresowes Ashton, **Helston**, TR13 9SY
01736 763299

Parc Mean B & B
Penrose Estate, **Helston**, TR13 ORB
01326 574290

Halftides B & B
Mullion Cove, **Helston**, TR12 7HU
01326 241935
http://www.halftides.co.uk
Halftides is a tranquil, peaceful hideaway situated within three acres, with stunning views towards Mullion Island and harbour.

Chydane B & B
Gunwalloe Fishing Cove, **Helston**, TR12 7QB
07941 232622
http://www.chydane.co.uk/
Luxury self-catering home with stunning sea views.

Treleague B & B
St Keverne, **Helston**, TR12 6PQ
01326 281500

The Hen House B & B
Tregarne, Manaccan, **Helston**, TR12 6EW
01326 280236
http://www.thehenhouse-cornwall.co.uk

Old Vicarage B & B
Mullion, TR12 7DQ
01326 240898

Quiet & peaceful B&B.

Tremenhere Cottage B & B
Coverack, **The Lizard**, TR12 6RD
01326 281531
http://tremenhere.idmpreview.co.uk
A Cornish stone cottage hidden in peaceful, tranquil countryside...

Landewednack House B & B
Church Cove, **The Lizard**, TR12 7PQ
01326 290877
http://www.landewednackhouse.com
Grade II listed it was originally a rectory and dates from 1683.

PUBS/GASTROPUBS

Above average pubs serving quality real ale, excellent bar food or both.

Halzephron Inn PUB
Gunwalloe, **Helston**, TR12 7QB
01326 240406
http://www.halzephron-inn.co.uk/
Located near the idyllic fishing village of Gunwalloe on the Lizard peninsula and affording breathtaking views all around.

Cadgwith Cove Inn PUB
Cadgwith, **Helston**, TR12 7JX
01326 290513
http://www.cadgwithcoveinn.com/
Offers a warm and traditional Cornish welcome. Tranquillity, beautifully rugged scenery, authentic local colour and seafaring tradition.

Halzephron GASTRO PUB
Gunwalloe, **Helston**, TR12 7QB
01326 240406
http://www.halzephron-inn.co.uk/

CHURCHES

These churches all have something special and are worthy of a visit. Star ratings are from Simon Jenkin's Best Churches.

St Winwaloe ★★☆☆☆ CHURCH
N of Lizard on Coast, **Gunwalloe**, TR12 7QA

St Breaca ★☆☆☆☆ CHURCH
Breage, **Helston**, TR13 9PL

St Mellanus ★☆☆☆☆ CHURCH
N of Lizard on coast, **Mullion**, TR12 7HE

HOUSES & CASTLES

Godolphin House ★★☆☆☆ HOUSE
Godolphin Cross, **Helston**, TR13 9RE
01736 763194
www.nationaltrust.org.uk/godolphin/
A historic house and medieval garden all set within an ancient and atmospheric estate

GARDENS

Gardens listed here have been rated by the "Good Gardens Guide".

Bosahan Garden GARDEN
Manaccan, **Helston**, TR12 6JL
01326 231351
http://www.gardensofcornwall.com/outdoor-kids/bosahan-garden-p465413
Close to the Helford River, Bosahan serves-up horticultural bliss with a breathtaking view to the estuary and sea. Bosahan has its own microclimate, enabling a fusion of tender plants from both hemispheres to flourish in the moist shelter. Radiant rows of rhododendrons and azaleas are mixed with the likes of magnolias and southern hemisphere tree and shrub species. The exotic palm groves and mature Maidenhair trees have made a lush canopy under which to explore the 'sub-tropical' environment. Bosahan is blessed with a meandering stream trickling through the centre, creating a wonderful garden for walkers to follow a trail along the fern-edged banks and palm-fringed pond.

Bonython Estate Gardens ★☆☆☆☆ GARDEN
Cury Cross Lanes, **Helston**, TR12 7BA
01326 240234
http://www.bonythonmanor.co.uk/
Remodeled in recent years, to include a contemporary water feature behind the delightful Georgian Manor, an eighteenth century Walled Garden, a Traditional Potager Garden, and an orchard of Cornish variety apple trees, on through parkland to a series of small lakes in a sheltered valley. Each lake has a different atmosphere and planting. Tranquillity, from the specimen trees and shrubs reflected in the water;

vibrant colour, from the hot, South African summer garden and exotic, from the mysterious quarry lake, a fernery and surrounding bamboos.

BEACHES

All of our beaches have the stamp of approval from the Marine Conservation Society (http://www.mcsuk.org/).

Praa Sands East & West BEACH
Helston, TR20 9RD
Mile long sand lifeguarded

Porthleven West BEACH
Helston, TR13 9EN
Mainly shingle lifeguarded

Poldu Cove BEACH
Helston, TR12 7BP
Sand lifeguarded

Polurrian Cove BEACH
Mullion, TR12 7EN
Sand lifeguarded

ARCHAEOLOGY

Halliggye ARCHAEOLOGY
Helston, TR12 6AH

Halliggye is a good example of a large well preserved Cornish fogou or underground chamber.

FAMILY FUN

National Seal Sanctuary FAMILY FUN
Gweek, **Helston**, TR12 6UG
01326 221361
http://www.sealsanctuary.co.uk
The Cornish Seal Sanctuary is set in the picturesque Helford Estuary, by the beautiful village of Gweek, in Cornwall. The Sanctuary is a busy rescue centre, and also has resident Grey Seals, Common Seals, Fur Seals, Patagonian & California Sea Lions, Penguins, Otters, Goats, Sheep and Ponies.

Poldark Mine FAMILY FUN
Wendron, **Helston**, TR13 0ER
01326 573173
http://www.poldark-mine.co.uk
Poldark has craft workshops run by local crafts people including jewellers, candle makers, pottery makers, ceramic painters and wood turners. Poldark is by far Cornwall's most popular mining heritage site.

Roswick Farm FAMILY FUN
Friendly camels, **Helston**,

Flambards Village Theme Park FAMILY FUN
Adult & child appeal - off A394, S edge of Helston, **Helston**, TR13 0QA
01326 573404
http://www.flambards.co.uk

GOLF COURSES

Courses in this guide have reached a very good standard and have something special to offer the advanced and novice player alike.

Mullion Golf Club ★★☆☆☆ GOLF
Cury, **Helston**, TR12 7BP
01326 240685
www.mulliongolfclub.co.uk/
Mullion Golf Club is situated on the cliffs of the Lizard Peninsula is not only the most southerly course in England, but one of the most beautiful courses in the West Country.

St Ives and Newlyn

St Ives and Newlyn have played a major role in British modern art which is why we mention them together though Newlyn is contiguous with Penzance, not St Ives. Though even earlier painters had kindled an interest in Cornwall, once the Saltash Bridge had connected Cornwall to the railway system, artists preceded tourists in taking advantage. The 'plein-air' (painting in the open air) movement started in Normandy and Brittany whence some Britons there brought it to Newlyn in the 1880's. The Franco-Irish Stanhope Forbes settled in Newlyn and his painting 'A Fish Sale on a Cornish Beach'(1885) caused a sensation at the Royal Academy and put this fishing village on the cultural map.. By 1900 some of the colony had drifted up to St Ives where the accent was on seascape rather than the social realism of the Newlyn school. In 1939 Ben Nicholson arrived in St Ives with his third wife Barbara Hepworth. They divorced in 1947 but she stayed on to become a world famous sculptress*, and her friend Bernard Leach, the no less famous potter. The Nicholson era was a high point in British abstractionism. Now, the Newlyn School headed by a major talent, Henry Garfit, is taking the action back to where it began over a century ago.

The story of these two towns, a score or more of famous names, and their impact on art, not just in Britain, is the subject of books and learned articles – this is barely an intro, but The Tate Gallery is in St Ives for a good reason and is one of the finest in the land for modern art, so is Barbara Hepworth's Sculpture Garden. The work of the Newlyn painters is best seen at the Penlees Gallery in Penzance. Chapel Street has some good buildings, especially the flamboyant Egyptian House

St Ives, pop. 10,000 is a delightful town, the seaside of the imagination. It also has a few unusually excellent restaurants. Godrevy Lighthouse on the horizon was the inspiration for Virginia Woolf's 'To the Lighthouse'. She spent some summer holidays here and many think it her finest novel.

*Single Form is the name of her most significant commission and

stands in the UN Plaza in New York City.

Carbis Bay near St Ives

St Ives and Newlyn

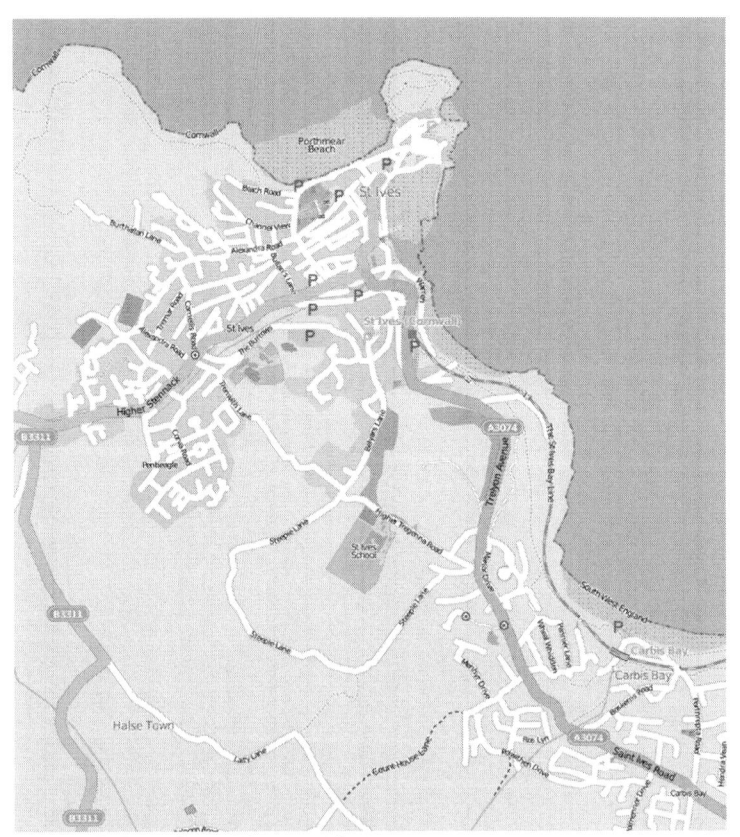

St Ives © OpenStreetMap contributors

OUR FAVOURITES

Blue Hayes, St Ives (TR26 2AD) HOTEL

Small boutique Private Hotel in St Ives - large ballustraded terrace with stunning views of the harbour and bay. Situated above Porthminster Beach, you can walk directly from the garden down the coastal path to the beach below, and along into the harbour in about ten minutes. Just six luxurious and spacious rooms - some with balcony, roof terrace or patio, all with fully-tiled en-suite bathrooms, with baths and showers with body jets. Licensed Cocktail Bar, private Dining Room, and on-site car parking. VisitBritain 3 Star Hotel with GOLD and BREAKFAST Awards.

Trelyon Avenue, **St Ives**, TR26 2AD
01736 797129
http://www.bluehayes.co.uk

Blas Burger Works, St Ives (TR26 2EA)
RESTAURANT

In this quirky, little beachside joint Blas has been notching up awards for many years now, primarily for the stance they take on environmental awareness and ethical, local sourcing. They achieved Cornwall's first 3 star rating from The Sustainable Restaurant Association, have two consecutive GOLD awards from The Green Tourism Business Scheme and have been listed for their 6th consecutive year in The Good Food Guide 2013. With it's shared tables, cardboard box seating and funky decor Blas offers "Burgers for people who give a damn".

The Warren, **St Ives**, TR26 2EA
01736 797272
http://www.blasburgerworks.co.uk

HOTELS

A selection of superior hotels, big or small, where you can be assured of quality, comfort and a warm welcome.

Boskerris Hotel `HOTEL`
Carbis Bay, **St Ives**, TR26 2NQ
01736 795295
http://www.boskerrishotel.co.uk

Blue Hayes `HOTEL`
Trelyon Avenue, **St Ives**, TR26 2AD
01736 797129
http://www.bluehayes.co.uk

Primrose Valley Hotel `HOTEL`
Porthminster Beach, **St Ives**, TR26 2ED
01736 794939
http://www.primroseonline.co.uk

The Gurnard's Head ★★★☆☆ `HOTEL`
Treen Nr Zennor, **Zennor**, TR26 3DE
01736 796928
http://www.gurnardshead.co.uk

BED & BREAKFAST

Interesting and highly rated B&Bs with a focus on your comfort and a warm welcome.

Calize Country House B & B
Gwithian, **Hayle**, TR27 5BW
01736 753268
http://www.calize.co.uk
Built in the 1870's for Lord Hocking, it has fabulous views across to Godrevy Lighthouse and St Ives Bay.

The Old Vicarage B & B
Brush End, **Lelant**, TR26 3EF
01736 753324
http://www.oldvicaragelelant.co.uk
Stylish self-catering accommodation - sleeps 14 people.

The Old Courthouse B & B
Lelant, TR26 3EB
01736 751798
http://www.oldcourthouse.cornwall.co.uk

Jamies Guest House B & B
Wheal Whidden, Carbis Bay, **St Ives**, TR26 2QX
01736 794718
All rooms at this thoughtful B&B have sea views over the bay.

Organic Panda B&B & gallery B & B
Pednolver Terrace, **St Ives**, TR26 2EL
01736 793890
http://www.organicpanda.co.uk
A boutique B&B in a beautiful location.

11 Sea View Terrace B & B
St Ives, TR26 2DH
01736 798440
http://www.11stives.co.uk/
Eleven Sea View Terrace is an Edwardian seaside villa offering elegant B&B.

The Old Count House B & B
1 Trenwith Square, **St Ives**, TR26 1DQ
01736 795369
http://www.theoldcounthouse-stives.co.uk/
The Old Count House is situated in a small, quiet square, the house enjoys breathtaking views of the town, harbour and bay.

House at Gwinear B & B
St Ives, TR27 5JZ
01736 850444

Tregeraint House B & B
Zennor, TR26 3DB
01736 797061
http://www.cornwall-online.co.uk/tregeraint-house/
A cornish cottage which has been turned into a comfortable B&B by potter Sue Wilson whilst retaining its traditional charm.

PUBS/GASTROPUBS

Above average pubs serving quality real ale, excellent bar food or both.

Gurnards Head Hotel ★★★☆☆ `PUB`
Zennor, TR26 3DE
01736 796928
http://www.gurnardshead.co.uk/
Cornwall Dining Pub of the Year

RESTAURANTS

Only top notch restaurants are listed here. Cooking stars are drawn from "The Good Food Guide 2013".

Alba Restaurant ★★★☆☆☆☆☆☆☆ RESTAURANT
Old Lifeboat House, Wharf Road, **St Ives**, TR26 1LF
01736 797222
http://www.thealbarestaurant.com
Ex-lifeboat house that lifts the spirits.

St Andrew Street Bistro ★☆☆☆☆☆☆☆☆☆ RESTAURANT
St Andrews Street, **St Ives**, TR26 1AH
01736 797470
http://www.bistrostives.co.uk
A bistro with an ever-changing and locally sourced menu.

Porthminster Beach Café ★★★☆☆☆☆☆☆☆ RESTAURANT
Porthminster Beach, **St Ives**, TR26 2EB
01736 795352
http://www.porthminstercafe.co.uk
Art Deco with adventurous Aussie at the stoves - very good.

The Black Rock ★★☆☆☆☆☆☆☆☆ RESTAURANT
Market Place, **St Ives**, TR26 1RZ
01736 791911
http://www.theblackrockstives.co.uk
Friendly and imaginative restaurant.

Seagrass Restaurant ★★☆☆☆☆☆☆☆☆
RESTAURANT

Fish Street, **St Ives**, TR26 1LT
01736 793763
www.seagrass-stives.com
Quality seafood, stylish setting.

Blas Burger Works ★☆☆☆☆☆☆☆☆☆
RESTAURANT

The Warren, **St Ives**, TR26 2EA
01736 797272
http://www.blasburgerworks.co.uk
Ronald Macdonald eat your heart out

Gurnard's Head ★★★☆☆☆☆☆☆☆ **RESTAURANT**
Zennor, TR26 3DE
01796 796928
http://www.gurnardshead.co.uk
Inkin name a guarantee of a certain sort of quirky quality.

CHURCHES

These churches all have something special and are worthy of a visit. Star ratings are from Simon Jenkin's Best Churches.

St Ives ★★☆☆☆ CHURCH
St Ives, TR26 1DS

St Senara ★☆☆☆☆ CHURCH
SW of St Ives, **Zennor**, TR26 3BS

GARDENS

Gardens listed here have been rated by the "Good Gardens Guide".

Barbara Hepworth Museum and Sculpture Garden
★☆☆☆☆ GARDEN

Barnoon Hill, **St Ives**, TR26 1AD
01736 796226
http://www.tate.org.uk/visit/tate-st-ives/barbara-hepworth-museum-and-sculpture-garden
Visiting the Barbara Hepworth Museum and Sculpture Garden is a unique experience that offers a remarkable insight into the work and outlook of one of Britain's most important twentieth century artists. Sculptures in bronze, stone and wood are on display in the museum and garden, along with paintings, drawings and archive material.

BEACHES

All of our beaches have the stamp of approval from the Marine Conservation Society (http://www.mcsuk.org/).

Porthmeor BEACH 🏁
St Ives, TR26 1JZ
Sand lifeguarded popular

Porth Kidney BEACH
St Ives, TR26 3
Sand lifeguarded

Porth Gwidden BEACH
St Ives, TR26 1NT
Sand, popular with children

Carbis Bay BEACH 🏁
St Ives, TR26 1JY
Golden sand. Lifeguarded.

Porthminster BEACH 🏁
St Ives, TR26 2EB
Sand lifeguarded best restaurant

The Towans Godrevy BEACH
St Ives, TR27 5ED
Sand rock lifeguarded

The Towans Hayle BEACH
St Ives, TR27 5AP
Expanse of sand lifeguarded

VIEWPOINTS

St Anthony VIEWPOINT
St Anthony, **St Ives**, TR2 5EZ
The village is situated on a peninsula between the Helford River and Gillan Harbour on the west side of Falmouth Bay.

MUSEUMS

Tate St Ives ★★★☆☆ MUSEUM
Porthmeor Beach, **St Ives**, TR26 1TG
01736 796226
http://www.tate.org.co.uk

Barbara Hepworth Museum & Sculpture Garden
★★★☆☆ MUSEUM
Barnoon Hill, **St Ives**, TR26 1AD
01736 796226
http://www.tate.org.co.uk

FAMILY FUN

Paradise Park Wildlife Sanctuary *FAMILY FUN*
Exotic birds & other rare animals, **Hayle**, TR27 4HB
01736 751020
http://www.paradisepark.org.uk

Wayside Folk Museum *FAMILY FUN*
Enjoyable local history inc wrecks, **Zennor**, TR26 3DA
01736 796945

NATURAL PRODUCE

Kelly's of Cornwall NATURAL PRODUCE
The Wharf, **St Ives**, PL31 1LP
01208 77277
http://www.kellysofcornwall.co.uk
Luxury Cornish ice creams

Matthew Stevens & Son NATURAL PRODUCE
Back Road East, St Ives, **St Ives**, TR26 3AR
01736 795135
http://www.mstevensandson.co.uk
Top wholesalers & retailers of fish & seafood

GOLF COURSES

Courses in this guide have reached a very good standard and have something special to offer the advanced and novice player alike.

West Cornwall Golf Club ★★★★☆ GOLF
Church Lane, Lelant, **St Ives**, TR26 3DZ
01736 753177
www.westcornwallgolfclub.co.uk/
West Cornwall Golf Club is one of the finest links courses in Cornwall. The course was established in 1889, making it the oldest Golf club in the Duchy and one that has won much acclaim.

ANTIQUES

Mike Read Antique Sciences ANTIQUES
1 Abbey Meadow, Lelant, **St Ives**, TR26 3LL
01736 757237

Tremayne Applied Arts ANTIQUES
Street-an-Pol, **St Ives**, TR26 2DS
01736 797779

A regularly changing display of Twentieth Century Design Classics of Furniture, Ceramics, Glass, Jewellery, Paintings and Prints, together with Contemporary Works.

Penzance and surrounding area

Penzance has a population of 20,000, the same as Truro but no other similarity. The medieval town was largely razed by a Spanish raiding party in the 16th C so the style now is mostly Regency and Victorian. The ten day Golowan Festival in late June culminates in Mazey Day . The night before is the 'Serpent Dance' where the dancers weave intricate patterns going hand to hand. The children feature prominently on Mazey Day but between groups the bands perform – Highland Scottish Pipers and finally the Bagas Degol, the uniquely Cornish Band in a performance that proves Cornwall is really only itself. The Lido is a huge open air sea water swimming pool opened in 1935, closed in 1992 and reopened in 1994 – grandest of its type but still facing an uncertain future.
In front of Market House is the statue of Sir Humphrey Davy (1788 – 1829) a leading scientist of his day and the inventor of the Davy Lamp which enabled miners to see without igniting flammable gases.
The Scillonian III sails to St Mary's from Penzance.

Pendenis Castle, Penzance

Penzance and surrounding area

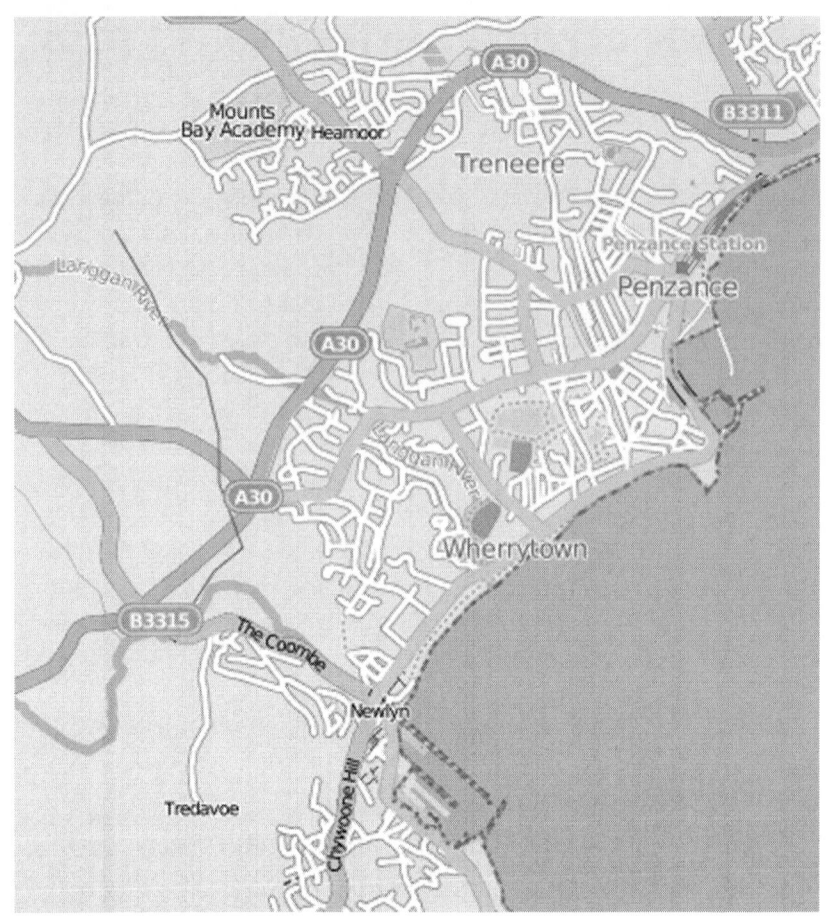

Penzance © OpenStreetMap contributors

HOTELS

A selection of superior hotels, big or small, where you can be assured of quality, comfort and a warm welcome.

Abbey Hotel HOTEL
Abbey Street, **Penzance**, TR18 4AR
01736 366906
http://www.theabbeyonline.co.uk

Hotel Penzance HOTEL
Britons Hill, **Penzance**, TR18 3AE
01736 363117
http://www.hotelpenzance.com

Ennys HOTEL
Trewhella Lane, St Hilary, **Penzance**, TR20 9BZ
01736 740262
http://www.ennys.co.uk
Ennys offers luxury five-star guesthouse accommodation and weekly cottage rentals.

BED & BREAKFAST

Interesting and highly rated B&Bs with a focus on your comfort and a warm welcome.

Lombard House B & B
16 Regent Terrace, **Penzance**, TR18 4DW
01736 364897
http://www.lombardhousehotel.co.uk
Lombard House Hotel is a grade II listed building dating back to the early 18th century.

PUBS/GASTROPUBS

Above average pubs serving quality real ale, excellent bar food or both.

The Victoria Inn PUB
Peranuthnoe, **Penzance**, TR20 9NP
01736 710309
http://www.victoriainn-penzance.co.uk/
Award-wining food, fine wines, good local ales and ciders.

Turks Head PUB
Chapel Street, **Penzance**, TR18 4AF
01736 363093
http://www.turksheadpenzance.co.uk/
Real ales and excellent pub food.

The Coldstreamer Inn ★★☆☆☆ GASTRO PUB
Gulval, **Penzance**, TR18 3BB
01736 362072
www.coldstreamer-penzance.co.uk

RESTAURANTS

Only top notch restaurants are listed here. Cooking stars are drawn from "The Good Food Guide 2013".

The Bakehouse ★★★☆☆☆☆☆☆☆ RESTAURANT
Old Bakehouse Lane, Chapel Street, **Penzance**, TR18 4AE
01736 331331
http://www.bakehouserestaurant.co.uk
Serving fantastically fresh Cornish produce, cooked simply to let it's flavour and quality shine.

The Bay ★★★☆☆☆☆☆☆☆ RESTAURANT
Mount Prospect Hotel, Briton's Hill, **Penzance**, TR18 3AE
01736 366890
http://www.bay-penzance.co.uk
Modern extension to Hotel Penzance - welcoming

Harris's ★★☆☆☆☆☆☆☆☆ RESTAURANT
46 New Street, **Penzance**, TR18 2LZ
01736 364408
http://www.harrissrestaurant.co.uk
Old town centre favourite.

CHURCHES

These churches all have something special and are worthy of a visit. Star ratings are from Simon Jenkin's Best Churches.

St Maddern ★☆☆☆☆ CHURCH
W of Penzance, **Madron**, TR18 3JW

St Buriana ★★☆☆☆ CHURCH
SW of Penzance, **St Buryan**, TR19 6DY

Penzance and surrounding area

GARDENS

Gardens listed here have been rated by the "Good Gardens Guide".

Trengwainton Garden ★☆☆☆☆ GARDEN
Madron, **Penzance**, TR20 8RZ
01736 363148
www.nationaltrust.org.uk/trengwainton-garden/
Sheltered garden bursting with exotic trees and shrubs

Chygurno GARDEN
Lamorna, **Penzance**, TR19 6XH
01736 732153
http://www.gardensofcornwall.com/outdoor-kids/chygurno-p466183
Indulge your sights and senses in this dramatic garden carved into the cliff edge teetering over the stunning Lamorna Cove. From its staggering perch on the edge of the ocean, this waterside garden tiers down in steep steps and terraces to meet sheltered woodland. A striking range of vibrant species stands out against a rugged backdrop, and as well as the spectacular sea view, Chygurno also boasts a unique decked vantage point that puts you on eye level with the treetops.

Trewidden Garden ★☆☆☆☆ GARDEN
Trewidden, **Penzance**, TR19 6AU
01736 363021
trewiddengarden.co.uk/
A maze of informal paths leads you around this peaceful Cornish garden with champion trees and shrubs, many of which are over 100 years old, to be discovered alongside some species of plants rarely seen grown in this country.

Tremenheere Sculpture Garden ★☆☆☆☆
GARDEN

Gulval, **Penzance**, TR20 8YL

www.tremenheere.co.uk/

Tremenheere Sculpture Gardens is a major new attraction in West Cornwall. In a beautiful sheltered valley, the woods, stream and dramatic vistas provide a perfect setting for large scale exotic and subtropical planting. Interwoven with this there is also an evolving programme of high quality contemporary art installations.

BEACHES

All of our beaches have the stamp of approval from the Marine Conservation Society (http://www.mcsuk.org/).

Porthcurno BEACH
Penzance, TR19 6JX
Fine white sand, lifeguarded

Sennen Cove BEACH
Penzance, TR19 7DG
Sand lifeguarded

Heliport Beach - Mounts Bay BEACH
Marazion, **Penzance**, TR17 0HQ
Sand lifegudarded

Mounts Bay Heliport BEACH
Penzance, TR18 3DP
Sand, lifeguarded. The beaches are formed by an expanse of hard sand backed by coastal protection walls of granite. The beach is popular with walkers and looks out to St Michael's Mount. A cycle path runs along the back of the beach.

ARCHAEOLOGY

Chysauster ARCHAEOLOGY
New Mill, **Penzance**, TR20 8LP

http://www.english-heritage.org.uk/daysout/properties/chysauster-ancient-village/
Chysauster Ancient Village is a late Iron Age and Romano-British village of courtyard houses. The village included eight to ten houses, each with its own internal courtyard. To the south east is the remains of a fogou, an underground structure of uncertain function.

MUSEUMS

Penlee House Gallery & Museum ★☆☆☆☆
MUSEUM

Morrab Road, **Penzance**, TR18 4HE
01736 363625
http://www.penleehouse.org.uk

FAMILY FUN

Salt Pilchard Works FAMILY FUN
Newlyn, TR18 5QH
01736 332112
http://www.pilchardworks.co.uk
The last Salt Pilchard works.

Lappa Valley Steam Railway & Leisure Park
FAMILY FUN

Newlyn East, **Newlyn East**, TR8 5LX
01872 510317
http://www.lappavalley.co.uk

Chysauster Ancient Village ★☆☆☆☆ FAMILY FUN
Newmill, **Penzance**, TR20 8XA
07831 757934
http://www.english-heritage.org.uk/daysout/properties/chysauster-ancient-village/
The village consisted of stone-walled homesteads known as 'courtyard houses', found only on the Land's End peninsula and the Isles of Scilly. The houses line a 'village street', and each had an open central courtyard surrounded by a number of thatched rooms. There are also the remains of an enigmatic 'fogou' underground passage.

Penzance and surrounding area

NATURAL PRODUCE

The Pilchard Works NATURAL PRODUCE
Tolcarne, **Newlyn**, TR18 5QH
01736 332112
http://pilchardworks.co.uk/
Traditional Cornish Pilchards and mackerel.

GOLF COURSES

Courses in this guide have reached a very good standard and have something special to offer the advanced and novice player alike.

Cape Cornwall Golf & Country Club ★☆☆☆☆
GOLF

St Just, **Penzance**, TR19 9NL
01736 788611
www.capecornwallgolfclub.co.uk/
Cape Cornwall Golf & Leisure is a truly unique place to relax, dine, or enjoy a game of golf on Britain's first and last 18 hole course.

ANTIQUES

Antiques & Fine Art ANTIQUES
1- 3 Queen's Buildings, The Promenade, **Penzance**, TR18 4HH
01736 350509

Penwith - The Western tip of Cornwall

Chysauster is off the B3311 Penzance - St Ives road. It is the best preserved Iron (tin here?) Age village in England , 200 BC, with the shells of eight stone buildings and their courtyards. Hut Six has the most obvious plan and is well worth the bracing walk.

Mousehole (Mowzle) is ur-picturesque and much given to holiday homes. Keigwin House is the only survivor of a Spanish raid in1595 and so is the oldest building . The Old Coastguard hotel and restaurant is the third enterprise of the Inkin brothers, after Gurnard's Head and one in Breconshire. The Christmas lights are widely renowned, very different from but roughly on the scale of Oxford Street. Park before you get there.

Marazion & St Michael's Mount is only 400 yds from the shore by causeway at low tide and small ferries otherwise. St Michael is the patron saint of high places but it has more than a name in common with its Norman namesake to which an older abbey founded by Edward the Confessor was granted by the Conqueror. The Cornish version is less grand than the Norman one which is visited by 3,000,000 people a year. So perhaps we should be pleased to let them take the hoards while we enjoy our more modest version in greater peace. There are four rooms worth seeing and a chapel. From the Garrison Room the Armada was first sighted and a beacon fire lit to spread the alarm.

Minack Theatre is atop a cliff 200 feet above the sea. An amphitheatre has been carved out of the rock in the open air and on the right evening it has real magic, so it is very hard to get tickets, even when the weather is bad.

Cape Cornwall north of Land's End was bought for the nation by the H J Heinz company for the nation and they erected the chimney on it in 1864. It now belongs to the NT. Some say it is the only proper cape in England because it divides the waters between the Irish Sea and the Atlantic. True or not, it is undoubtedly a more romantic place than Land's End.

Land's End has majesty you might expect from England's extreme western tip and you will feel this if you arrive by the South West Coast Path on foot. Otherwise you will struggle to find a reason for being there.

St Michael's Mount

Penwith - The Western tip of Cornwall

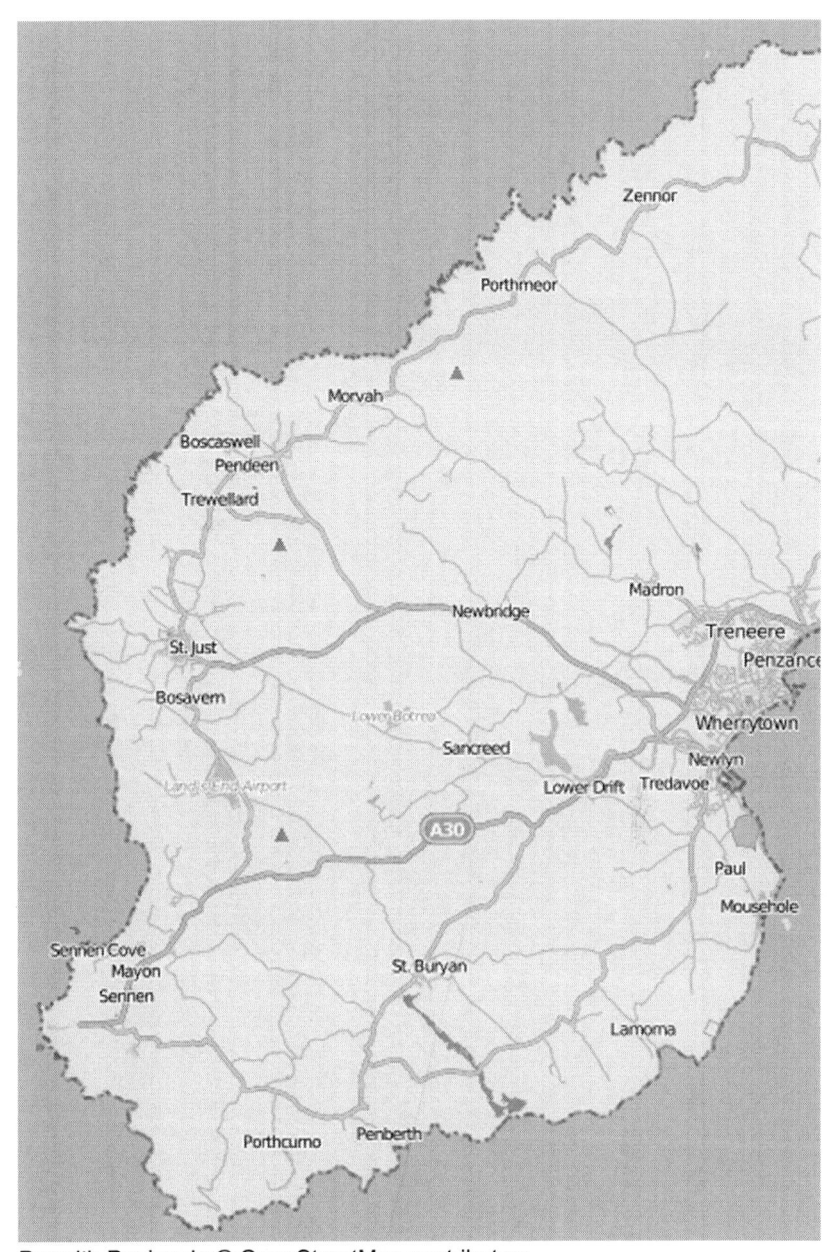

Penwith Peninsula © OpenStreetMap contributors

Penwith - The Western tip of Cornwall

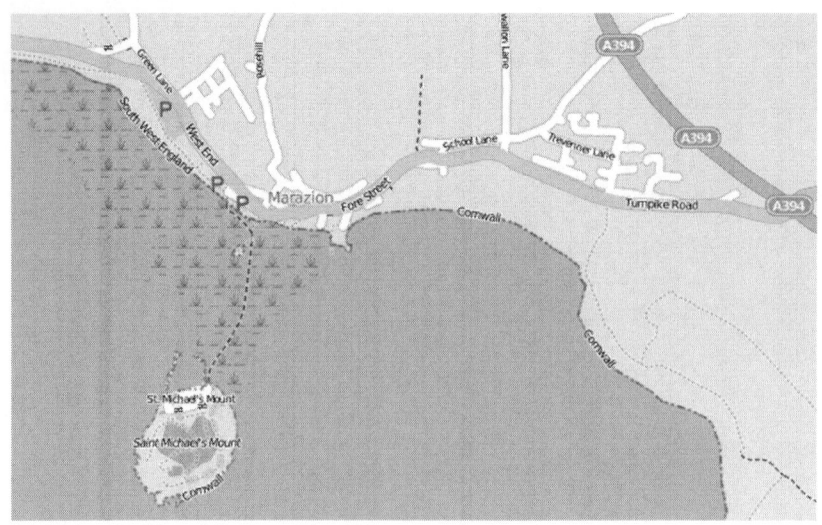

St Michael's Mount © OpenStreetMap contributors

OUR FAVOURITES

Mount Haven Hotel, Marazion (TR17 0DQ) HOTEL

A small boutique hotel with 18 rooms. Wonderful food, lovely staff and one treatment room - offering a unique 'Time to Transform' experience. Everyone can book one-off treatments, guests and non-residents as well.

Turnpike Road, **Marazion**, TR17 0DQ
01736 710249
http://www.mounthaven.co.uk

HOTELS

A selection of superior hotels, big or small, where you can be assured of quality, comfort and a warm welcome.

Mount Haven Hotel HOTEL
Turnpike Road, **Marazion**, TR17 0DQ
01736 710249
http://www.mounthaven.co.uk

Talland Bay Hotel HOTEL
Porthhallow, PL13 2JB
01503 272667
http://www.tallandbayhotel.co.uk

Penwith - The Western tip of Cornwall

BED & BREAKFAST

Interesting and highly rated B&Bs with a focus on your comfort and a warm welcome.

Seawitch cottage B & B
Chapel Road, **Leedstown**, TR27 6BA
01736 850917

Very comfortable self-catering accomodation.

Treglisson B & B
Wheal Alfred Road, **Leedstown**, TR27 5JT
01736 753141
http://www.treglisson.co.uk
With attractive gardens and indoor heated swimming pool.

Ednovean farm B & B
Perranuthnoe, TR20 9LZ
01736 711883
http://www.ednoveanfarm.co.uk
Ednovean Farm a is peaceful 17 century farmstead offering 5* B&B.

PUBS/GASTROPUBS

Above average pubs serving quality real ale, excellent bar food or both.

Old Coastguard `PUB`

The Parade, **Mousehole**, TR19 6PR
01736 731222
http://www.oldcoastguardhotel.co.uk/
Cornwall Dining Pub of the Year. Great position, civilized & friendly.

RESTAURANTS

Only top notch restaurants are listed here. Cooking stars are drawn from "The Good Food Guide 2013".

2 Fore Street ★★☆☆☆☆☆☆☆☆ RESTAURANT

Mousehole, TR19 6QU
01736 731164
http://www.2forestreet.co.uk
A chic and stylish French bistro-style restaurant on Mousehole harbour front.

The Old Coastguard ★★★☆☆☆☆☆☆☆ RESTAURANT

The Parade, **Mousehole**, TR19 6PR
01736 731222

Now part of the Inkin bros. family.

Victoria Inn ★★☆☆☆☆☆☆☆☆ RESTAURANT

Perranuthnoe, TR20 9NP
01736 710309
http://www.victoriainn-penzance.co.uk
Ancient inn, appealing cooking.

Kota ★★☆☆☆☆☆☆☆☆ RESTAURANT

Harbour Head, **Porthleven**, TR13 9JA
01326 562407
http://www.kotarestaurant.co.uk
Inventive racy flavours

CHURCHES

These churches all have something special and are worthy of a visit. Star ratings are from Simon Jenkin's Best Churches.

St Levan ★☆☆☆☆ CHURCH
By the Minack open air theatre, **St Levan**, TR19 6LH

BEACHES

All of our beaches have the stamp of approval from the Marine Conservation Society (http://www.mcsuk.org/).

Kennack Sands BEACH
Kuggar, TR12 7LT
Sand. Lifeguarded. Just outside the village of Kuggar on the Lizard Peninsula, is well known amoungst the surfing fraternity. This beach has a big tidal range due to its shallow angle and regularly throws up 4 to 5 foot waves.

Perran Sands BEACH
Perranuthnoe, TR26 9NE
Sand, novice surfing

Portreath Beach BEACH
Portreath, PL26 6TE
Sand, shingle, lifeguarded

VIEWPOINTS

Cape Cornwall VIEWPOINT
St Just, TR19 7NN

A cape is the point of land where two bodies of water meet and until the first Ordnance Survey, 200 years ago, it was thought that Cape Cornwall was the most westerly point in Cornwall. Most of the headland is owned by the National Trust. There is also a National Coastwatch look out on the seaward side. The only tourist infrastructure at present is a car park (owned by the National Trust) and a public toilet and refreshments van during the summer.

ARCHAEOLOGY

Lanyon Quoit ARCHAEOLOGY
Morvah, TR20 8NZ

Lanyon Quoit is a dolmen in Cornwall, 2 miles southeast of Morvah. It stands next to the road leading from Madron to Morvah. In the 18th century, the structure was tall enough for a person on horse back to stand under. The capstone rested at 7 feet high with dimensions of 9 feet by 17.5 feet weighing 13.5 tons. The monument is thought to be a burial chamber; perhaps a mausoleum.

Carn Euny ARCHAEOLOGY
Sancreed, TR20 8QZ

http://www.english-heritage.org.uk/daysout/properties/carn-euny-ancient-village

Carn Euny is an archaeological site near Sancreed, on the Penwith peninsula with considerable evidence of both Iron Age and post-Iron Age settlement. Excavations on this site have shown that there was activity at Carn Euny as early as the Neolithic period. There is evidence that shows that the first timber huts in this site were built around 200 BC, but by the 1st century before Christ, these timber huts had been replaced by stone huts. The remains of these stone huts are still visible today.

Carn Euny is best known for the well-preserved state of the large fogou, an underground passageway, which is more than 65 feet (20 metres) long. This fogou runs just below the surface of the ground and is roofed with massive stone slabs. Although the exact purpose of these fogous is still a mystery, possibilities include storage, habitation, or ritual. The site was abandoned late in the Roman period.

Merry Maidens ARCHAEOLOGY
St Buryan, TR19 6BQ

The Merry Maidens, also known as Dawn's Men (a likely corruption of the Cornish Dans Maen "Stone Dance") is a late neolithic stone circle located 2 miles to the south of the village of St Buryan.

Zennor Quoit ARCHAEOLOGY
Zennor, TR26 3BP

Zennor Quoit is a ruined megalithic burial chamber or dolmen, located on a moor about a mile east of the village of Zennor on the Penwith peninsular. It dates to 2500–1500 BC. Apart from the fallen roof, the chamber is in good condition.

FAMILY FUN

Land's End `FAMILY FUN`
Wonderful coastal walks in both directions
http://www.landsend-landmark.co.uk

St Michael's Mount ★★★☆☆ `FAMILY FUN`
Marazion, TR17 0HS
01736 710507
www.stmichaelsmount.co.uk/
Stroll across the causeway where a legendary giant once walked. Follow the footsteps of pilgrims. Boat hop to an island where modern life meets layers of history. Discover a medieval castle, a sub-tropical paradise and a close-knit island community. Delve into the history of a fortress, a priory, a harbour and a home.

Geevor Tin Mine `FAMILY FUN`
Pendeen, TR19 7EW
01736 788662
http://www.geevor.com

Minack Theatre `FAMILY FUN`
Porthcurno, TR19 6JU
01736 810181
http://www.minack.com
The Minack Theatre is Cornwall's world famous open-air theatre. The SUMMER SEASON of theatre runs from May to September presenting drama, musicals and opera in this most dramatic of settings. Visit during the day and explore this world famous open-air theatre created from a cliffside at Porthcurno by Rowena Cade. The SUB-TROPICAL GARDENS have become an established favourite, especially for gardeners with a taste for the exotic. The plants thrive on the open cliffside providing a dash of colour to the Minack all year round.

NATURAL PRODUCE

Quayside Fish Centre NATURAL PRODUCE
The Harbourside, Porthleven, **Porthleven**, TR13 9JU
01326 562008
http://www.quaysidefish.co.uk
Award winning fishmonger

Send us a review and get a free ebook

We'd like to make The Good Guide to Cornwall even better by featuring reviews by real people. Can you help?

Have you visited any of the places featured in this guide? Would you like to have a review – your honest opinion – appear in these pages? Please email us a review at

review@thegoodguides.co.uk

If your review is featured in the next edition of this guide then we will gift you an ebook version of the good guide of your choice for free.

Sources

The **good guides** are a unique source of information for an area, for those seeking the best and keen to avoid disappointment.

This new concept is drawn from the sources listed here, supported by our own extensive knowledge of the area.

The Good Food Guide
The Good Pub Guide
The Good Hotel Guide
Alastair Sawday's British Bed & Breakfast
Wolsey Lodges
Britain's Finest
Unique Homestays
Good Gardens Guide
England's Thousand Best Churches — Simon Jenkins
England's Thousand Best Houses — Simon Jenkins
1000 Best Courses in Britain and Ireland — Golf World
Britain's Best Museums and Galleries — Mark Fisher
The Marine Conservation Society
and a wide range of regional specialists

The **only** single source of the best recommendations for everything you need for your trip.

Printed in Great Britain
by Amazon.co.uk, Ltd.,
Marston Gate.